THE
NEUROTIC PERSONALITY
OF OUR TIME

KAREN HORNEY, M.D.

THE NEUROTIC PERSONALITY OF OUR TIME

W · W · NORTON & COMPANY

New York · London

W. W. Norton & Company, Inc. is also the publisher of the
works of Erik H. Erikson, Otto Fenichel, Karen Horney, Harry Stack
Sullivan, and The Standard Edition of the Complete Psychological
Works of Sigmund Freud.

W. W. Norton & Company, Inc. 500 Fifth Avenue,
New York, N.Y. 10110

ISBN 0-393-00742-1

PRINTED IN THE UNITED STATES OF AMERICA
8 · 9 · 0

· CONTENTS ·

Contents

· INTRODUCTION ·

THE purpose I have had in mind in writing this book has been to give an accurate picture of the neurotic person who lives among us, with the conflicts which actually move him, with his anxieties, his suffering and the many difficulties he has in his relations with others as well as with himself. I am not concerned here with any particular type or types of neuroses, but have concentrated on the character structure which recurs in nearly all neurotic persons of our time in one or another form.

Emphasis is put on the actually existing conflicts and the neurotic's attempts to solve them, on his actually existing anxieties and the defenses he has built up against them. This emphasis on the actual situation does not mean that I discard the idea that essentially neuroses develop out of early childhood experiences. But I differ from many psychoanalytic writers inasmuch as I do not consider it justified to focus our attention on childhood in a sort of one-sided fascination and to consider later reactions essentially as repetitions of earlier ones. I want to show that the relation between childhood experiences and later conflicts is much more intricate than is assumed by those psychoanalysts who proclaim a simple cause and effect relationship. Though experiences in childhood provide determining conditions for neuroses they are nevertheless not the only cause of later difficulties.

Introduction

When we focus our attention on the actual neurotic difficulties we recognize that neuroses are generated not only by incidental individual experiences, but also by the specific cultural conditions under which we live. In fact the cultural conditions not only lend weight and color to the individual experiences but in the last analysis determine their particular form. It is an individual fate, for example, to have a domineering or a "self-sacrificing" mother, but it is only under definite cultural conditions that we find domineering or self-sacrificing mothers, and it is also only because of these existing conditions that such an experience will have an influence on later life.

When we realize the great import of cultural conditions on neuroses the biological and physiological conditions, which are considered by Freud to be their root, recede into the background. The influence of these latter factors should be considered only on the basis of well established evidence.

This orientation of mine has led to some new interpretations for a number of basic problems in neuroses. Though these interpretations refer to disparate questions such as the problem of masochism, the implications of the neurotic need for affection, the meaning of neurotic guilt feelings, they all have a common basis in an emphasis on the determining role that anxiety plays in bringing about neurotic character trends.

Since many of my interpretations deviate from those of Freud some readers may ask whether this is still psychoanalysis. The answer depends on what one holds essential in psychoanalysis. If one believes that it is constituted entirely by the sum total of theories propounded by Freud, then what is presented here is not psychoanalysis. If, however, one believes that the essentials of psychoanalysis lie in certain basic trends of thought concerning the role of unconscious processes and the ways in which they find expression, and in a form of therapeutic treatment that brings these processes to awareness, then what I present is psychoanalysis. I believe that a strict adherence to all of Freud's theoretical interpretations entails the danger of tending to find in neuroses what Freud's theories lead one to expect to find. It is the danger of stagnation. I believe that deference for Freud's gigantic achievements should show itself in building on the foundations that he has laid, and that in this way we can help to fulfill the possibilities which psychoanalysis has for the future, as a theory as well as a therapy.

These remarks answer also another possible question: whether my interpretation is somewhat Adlerian. There are some similarities with certain points that Adler has stressed, but fundamentally my interpretation rests on Freudian ground. Adler is in fact a good example of how even a productive insight into psychological processes can become sterile if pursued onesidedly and without foundation in the basic discoveries of Freud.

Since it has not been the main purpose of this book to define in what respects I agree or disagree with other psychoanalytic writers, I have on the whole limited my discussion of polemic points to certain questions on which my opinions conspicuously diverge from those of Freud.

What I have presented here are the impressions I have gained in long psychoanalytic study of neuroses. To present the material on which my interpretations are based I should have had to include many detailed case histories, a procedure which would have been unduly cumbersome in a book intended to give a general presentation of problems in neuroses. Even without this material, however, it is possible for the specialist and even for the layman to test the validity of my statements. If he is an attentive observer he can compare my assumptions with his own observations and experience, and on this basis reject or accept, modify or underscore what I have said.

The book is written in plain language, and for the sake of clarity I have refrained from discussing too many ramifications. Technical terms have been avoided as much as possible because there is always the danger of letting such terms substitute for clear thinking. Thus it may appear to many readers, particularly laymen, that the problems of the neurotic personality are easily understood. But this would be a mistaken and even a dangerous conclusion. We cannot escape the fact that all psychological problems are necessarily profoundly intricate and subtle. If there is anyone who is not willing to accept this fact he is warned not to read the book lest he find himself in a maze and be disappointed in his search for ready formulae.

The book is addressed to the interested layman as well as to those who have to deal professionally with neurotic persons and are familiar with the problems involved. Among these it is intended not only for psychiatrists but for social workers and teachers, and also for those groups of anthropologists and sociologists who have become aware of the significance of psychic factors in the study of different cultures. Finally, I hope it will have some significance for the neurotic himself. If he does not on principle refute any psychological thinking as an intrusion and an imposition he often has on the basis of his own suffering a keener and finer understanding of psychological intricacies than his more robust brothers. Unfortunately reading about his situation will not cure him; in what he reads he may recognize others much more readily than himself.

I take this opportunity to express my thanks to Miss Elizabeth Todd, who has edited the book. The writers to whom I feel indebted are mentioned in the text. My main gratitude goes to Freud because he has provided us with the foundation and the tools to work with, and to my patients because whatever understanding I have has grown out of our work together.

· CHAPTER 1 ·

Cultural and Psychological Implications of Neuroses

WE USE the term "neurotic" quite freely today without always having, however, a clear conception of what it denotes. Often it is hardly more than a slightly highbrow way of expressing disapproval: one who formerly would have been content to say lazy, sensitive, demanding or suspicious, is now likely to say instead "neurotic." Yet we do have something in mind when we use the term, and without being quite aware of it we apply certain criteria to determine its choice.

First of all, neurotic persons are different from the average individuals in their reactions. We should be inclined to consider neurotic, for example, a girl who prefers to remain in the rank and file, refuses to accept an increased salary and does not wish to be identified with her superiors, or an artist who earns thirty dollars a week but could earn more if he gave more time to his work, and who prefers instead to enjoy life as well as he can on that amount, to spend a good deal of his time in the company of women or in indulging in technical hobbies. The reason we should call such persons neurotic is that most of us are familiar, and exclusively familiar, with a behavior pattern that implies wanting to get ahead in the world, to get ahead of others, to earn more money than the bare minimum for existence.

These examples show that one criterion we apply in

designating a person as neurotic is whether his mode of living coincides with any of the recognized behavior patterns of our time. If the girl without competitive drives, or at least without apparent competitive drives, lived in some Pueblo Indian culture, she would be considered entirely normal, or if the artist lived in a village in Southern Italy or in Mexico he, too, would be considered normal, because in those environments it is inconceivable that anyone should want to earn more money or to make any greater effort than is absolutely necessary to satisfy immediate needs. Going farther back, in Greece the attitude of wanting to work more than one's needs required would have been considered positively indecent.

Thus the term neurotic, while originally medical, cannot be used now without its cultural implications. One can diagnose a broken leg without knowing the cultural background of the patient, but one would run a great risk in calling an Indian boy [1] psychotic because he told us that he had visions in which he believed. In the particular culture of these Indians the experience of visions and hallucinations is regarded as a special gift, a blessing from the spirits, and they are deliberately induced as conferring a certain prestige on the person who has them. With us a person would be neurotic or psychotic who talked by the hour with his deceased grandfather, whereas such communication with ancestors is a recognized pattern in some Indian tribes. A person who felt mortally offended if the name of a deceased relative were mentioned we should consider neurotic indeed, but he would be absolutely normal in the

[1] *Cf.* H. Scudder Mekeel, "Clinic and Culture" in *Journal of Abnormal and Social Psychology*, vol. 30 (1935), pp. 292–300.

Jicarilla Apache culture.[2] A man mortally frightened by the approach of a menstruating woman we should consider neurotic, while with many primitive tribes fear concerning menstruation is the average attitude.

The conception of what is normal varies not only with the culture but also within the same culture, in the course of time. Today, for example, if a mature and independent woman were to consider herself "a fallen woman," "unworthy of the love of a decent man," because she had had sexual relationships, she would be suspected of a neurosis, at least in many circles of society. Some forty years ago this attitude of guilt would have been considered normal. The conception of normality varies also with the different classes of society. Members of the feudal class, for example, find it normal for a man to be lazy all the time, active only at hunting or warring, whereas a person of the small bourgeois class showing the same attitude would be considered decidedly abnormal. This variation is found also according to sex distinctions, as far as they exist in society, as they do in Western culture, where men and women are supposed to have different temperaments. For a woman to become obsessed with the dread of growing old as she approaches the forties is, again, "normal," while a man getting jittery about age at that period of life would be neurotic.

To some extent every educated person knows that there are variations in what is regarded as normal. We know that the Chinese eat foods different from ours; that the Eskimos have different conceptions of cleanliness; that the medicine-man has different ways of cur-

[2] M. E. Opler, "An Interpretation of Ambivalence of two American Indian Tribes" in *Journal of Social Psychology*, vol. 7 (1936), pp. 82–116.

ing the sick from those used by the modern physician. That there are, however, variations not only in customs but also in drives and feelings, is less generally understood, though implicitly or explicitly it has been stated by anthropologists.[3] It is one of the merits of modern anthropology, as Sapir [4] has put it, to be always rediscovering the normal.

For good reasons every culture clings to the belief that its own feelings and drives are the one normal expression of "human nature," [5] and psychology has not made an exception to this rule. Freud, for example, concludes from his observations that woman is more jealous than man, and then tries to account for this presumably general phenomenon on biological grounds.[6] Freud also seems to assume that all human beings ex-

---

[3] *Cf.* the excellent presentations of anthropological material in: Margaret Mead, *Sex and Temperament in Three Primitive Societies;* Ruth Benedict, *Patterns of Culture;* A. S. Hallowell's forthcoming book, *Handbook of Psychological Leads for Ethnological Field Workers.*

[4] Edward Sapir, "Cultural Anthropology and Psychiatry" in *Journal of Abnormal and Social Psychology,* vol. 27 (1932), pp. 229–242.

[5] *Cf.* Ruth Benedict, *Patterns of Culture.*

[6] In his paper "Some Psychological Consequences of the Anatomical Distinction between the Sexes" Freud propounds the theory that the anatomical sexual differences inevitably lead every girl to envy a boy his possession of the penis. Later on her wish to possess a penis is transformed to a wish to possess a man as the carrier of a penis. She then begrudges other women their relations with men—more accurately, their possession of men—as she originally had begrudged the boy his possession of a penis. In making statements like these Freud is yielding to the temptation of his time: to make generalizations about human nature for the whole of mankind, though his generalization grows from the observation of only one culture zone.

The anthropologist would not query the validity of Freud's observations; he would accept them as pertaining to a certain part of the population of a certain culture at a certain time. He would query, however, the validity of Freud's generalizations by pointing out that there exist endless differences among peoples concerning their attitudes toward jealousy, that there are peoples where men are more jealous than women, others where both sexes lack individual jealousy, others where both sexes are inordinately jealous. In view of these existing differences he would refute Freud's—or in fact anyone's—endeavor to account for his observations on the basis of anatomical sexual differences. Instead he would stress the necessity of investigating differences of life conditions and their influence on the development of jealousy in men or women. For our cul-

perience guilt feelings concerning murder.[7] It is an indisputable fact, however, that the greatest variations exist in the attitude toward killing. As Peter Freuchen has shown,[8] the Eskimos do not feel that a murderer requires punishment. In many primitive tribes the injury done a family when one of its members is killed by an outsider may be repaired by presenting a substitute. In some cultures the feelings of a mother whose son has been killed can be assuaged by adopting the murderer in his place.[9]

Making further use of anthropological findings we must recognize that some of our conceptions about human nature are rather naïve, for example the idea that competitiveness, sibling rivalry, kinship between affection and sexuality, are trends inherent in human nature. Our conception of normality is arrived at by the approval of certain standards of behavior and feeling within a certain group which imposes these standards upon its members. But the standards vary with culture, period, class and sex.

These considerations have more far-reaching implications for psychology than appears at first impression. The immediate consequence is a feeling of doubt about psychological omniscience. From resemblances between findings concerning our culture and those concerning

[7] Sigmund Freud, *Totem and Taboo.*
[8] Peter Freuchen, *Arctic Adventure and Eskimo.*
[9] Robert Briffault, *The Mothers.*

---

ture, for instance, it would have to be asked whether Freud's observation, which holds true for neurotic women of our culture, applies also to normal women of this culture. This question has to be raised because frequently psychoanalysts, who have to deal day after day with neurotic persons, lose sight of the fact that normal persons, too, exist in our culture. It would also have to be asked, what are the psychological conditions that make for an enhanced jealousy or possessiveness concerning the other sex, and what are the differences in the life conditions of men and women in our culture that account for a difference in the development of jealousy.

other cultures we must not conclude that both are due to the same motivations. It is no longer valid to suppose that a new psychological finding reveals a universal trend inherent in human nature. The effect of all this is to confirm what some sociologists have repeatedly asserted: that there is no such thing as a normal psychology, which holds for all mankind.

These limitations, however, are more than compensated by the opening up of new possibilities of understanding. The essential implication of these anthropological considerations is that feelings and attitudes are to an amazingly high degree molded by the conditions under which we live, both cultural and individual, inseparably interwoven. This in turn means that if we know the cultural conditions under which we live we have a good chance of gaining a much deeper understanding of the special character of normal feelings and attitudes. And inasmuch as neuroses are deviations from the normal pattern of behavior there is for them, too, a prospect of better understanding.

In part, taking this way means following Freud along the path that led him ultimately to present the world with a hitherto unthought-of understanding of neuroses. While in theory Freud traced back our peculiarities to biologically-given drives he has emphatically represented the opinion—in theory and still more in practice—that we cannot understand a neurosis without a detailed knowledge of the individual's life circumstances, particularly the molding influences of affection in early childhood. Applying the same principle to the problem of normal and neurotic structures in a given culture means that we cannot understand these structures without a detailed knowledge of the influences the particular culture exerts over the individual.[10]

For the rest it means that we have to take a definite step beyond Freud, a step which is possible, though, only on the basis of Freud's revealing discoveries. For although in one respect he is far ahead of his own time, in another—in his over-emphasis on the biological origin of mental characteristics—Freud has remained rooted in its scientific orientations. He has assumed that the instinctual drives or object relationships that are frequent in our culture are biologically determined "human nature" or arise out of unalterable situations (biologically given "pregenital" stages, Oedipus complex).

Freud's disregard of cultural factors not only leads to false generalizations, but to a large extent blocks an understanding of the real forces which motivate our attitudes and actions. I believe that this disregard is the main reason why psychoanalysis, inasmuch as it faithfully follows the theoretical paths beaten by Freud, seems in spite of its seemingly boundless potentialities to have come into a blind alley, mani-

[10] Many writers have recognized the importance of cultural factors as a determining influence in psychological conditions. Erich Fromm, in his paper "Zur Entstehung des Christusdogmas" in *Imago*, vol. 16 (1930), pp. 307–373, was the first in German psychoanalytic literature to present and elaborate this method of approach. Later it was taken up by others, such as Wilhelm Reich and Otto Fenichel. In the United States Harry Stack Sullivan was the first to see the necessity for psychiatry to consider cultural implications. Other American psychiatrists who have viewed the problem in this way include Adolf Meyer, William A. White (*Twentieth Century Psychiatry*), William A. Healy and Augusta Bronner (*New Light on Delinquency*). Recently some psychoanalysts, such as F. Alexander and A. Kardiner, have become interested in the cultural implications of psychological problems. Among the social scientists with this point of view *cf.* especially H. D. Lasswell (*World Politics and Personal Insecurity*) and John Dollard (*Criteria for the Life History*).

festing itself in a rank growth of abstruse theories and the use of a shadowy terminology.

We have seen now that a neurosis involves deviation from the normal. This criterion is very important, though it is not sufficient. Persons may deviate from the general pattern without having a neurosis. The artist cited above, who refused to give more time than necessary to earning money, may have a neurosis or he may simply be wise in not permitting himself to be pulled into the current of competitive struggle. On the other hand, many persons may have a severe neurosis who according to surface observation are adapted to existing patterns of life. It is in such cases that the psychological or medical point of view is necessary.

Curiously enough, it is anything but easy to say what constitutes a neurosis from this point of view. At any rate, as long as we study the manifest picture alone, it is difficult to find characteristics common to all neuroses. We certainly cannot use the symptoms—such as phobias, depressions, functional physical disorders—as a criterion, because they may not be present. Inhibitions of some sort are always present, for reasons I shall discuss later, but they may be so subtle or so well disguised as to escape surface observation. The same difficulties would arise if we should judge from the manifest picture alone the disturbances in relations with other people, including the disturbances in sexual relations. These are never missing but they may be very difficult to discern. There are two characteristics, however, which one may discern in all neuroses without having an intimate knowledge of the personality structure: a certain rigidity in reaction and a discrepancy between potentialities and accomplishments.

Both characteristics need further explanation. By rigidity in reactions I mean a lack of that flexibility which enables us to react differently to different situations. The normal person, for instance, is suspicious where he senses or sees reasons for being so; a neurotic person may be suspicious, regardless of the situation, all the time, whether he is aware of his state or not. A normal person is able to discriminate between compliments meant sincerely and those of an insincere nature; the neurotic person does not differentiate between the two or may discount them altogether, under all conditions. A normal person will be spiteful if he feels an unwarranted imposition; a neurotic may react with spite to any insinuation, even if he realizes that it is in his own interest. A normal person may be undecided, at times, in a matter important and difficult to decide; a neurotic may be undecided at all times.

Rigidity, however, is indicative of a neurosis only when it deviates from the cultural patterns. A rigid suspicion of anything new or strange is a normal pattern among a large proportion of peasants in Western civilization; and the small bourgeois' rigid emphasis on thrift is also an example of normal rigidity.

In the same way, a discrepancy between the potentialities of a person and his actual achievements in life may be due only to external factors. But it is indicative of a neurosis if in spite of gifts and favorable external possibilities for their development the person remains unproductive; or if in spite of having all the possibilities for feeling happy he cannot enjoy what he has; or if in spite of being beautiful a woman feels that she cannot attract men. In other words, the neurotic has the impression that he stands in his own way.

Leaving aside the manifest picture and looking at the dynamics effective in producing neuroses, there is one essential factor common to all neuroses, and that is anxieties and the defenses built up against them. Intricate as the structure of a neurosis may be, this anxiety is the motor which sets the neurotic process going and keeps it in motion. The meaning of this statement will become clear in the following chapters, and therefore I refrain from citing examples now. But even if it is to be accepted only tentatively as a basic principle it requires elaboration.

As it stands the statement is obviously too general. Anxieties or fears—let us use these terms interchangeably for a while—are ubiquitous, and so are defenses against them. These reactions are not restricted to human beings. If an animal, frightened by some danger, either makes a counter-attack or takes flight, we have exactly the same situation of fear and defense. If we are afraid of being struck by lightning and put a lightning-rod on our roof, if we are afraid of the consequences of possible accidents and take out an insurance policy, the factors of fear and defense are likewise present. They are present in various specific forms in every culture, and may be institutionalized, as in the wearing of amulets as a defense against the fear of the evil eye, the observation of circumstantial rites against the fear of the dead, the taboos concerning the avoidance of menstruating women as a defense against the fear of evil emanating from them.

These similarities present a temptation to make a logical error. If the factors of fear and defense are essential in neuroses, why not call the institutionalized defenses against fear the evidence of "cultural" neuroses? The fallacy in reasoning this way lies in the fact that two phenomena are not necessarily identical when they have one element in common. One would not call a house a rock merely because it is built out of the same material as a rock. What, then, is the characteristic of neurotic fears and defenses that makes them specifically neurotic? Is it perhaps that the neurotic fears are imaginary? No, for we might also be inclined to call fear of the dead imaginary; and in both cases we should be yielding to an impression based on lack of understanding. Is it perhaps that the neurotic essentially does not know why he is afraid? No, for neither does the primitive know why he has a fear of the dead. The distinction has nothing to do with gradations of awareness or rationality, but it consists in the following two factors.

First, life conditions in every culture give rise to some fears. They may be caused by external dangers (nature, enemies), by the forms of social relationships (incitement to hostility because of suppression, injustice, enforced dependence, frustrations), by cultural traditions (traditional fear of demons, of violation of taboos) regardless of how they may have originated. An individual may be subject more or less to these fears, but on the whole it is safe to assume that they are thrust upon every individual living in a given culture, and that no one can avoid them. The neurotic, however, not only shares the fears common to all individuals in a culture, but because of conditions in his individual life—which, however, are interwoven with general conditions—he also has fears which in quantity or quality deviate from those of the cultural pattern.

Secondly, the fears existing in a given culture are warded off in general by certain protective devices (such as taboos, rites, customs). As a rule these defenses represent a more economical way of dealing with fears than do the neurotic's defenses built up in a different way. Thus the normal person, though having to undergo the fears and defenses of his culture, will in general be quite capable of living up to his potentialities and of enjoying what life has to offer to him. The normal person is capable of making the best of the possibilities given in his culture. Expressing it negatively, he does not suffer more than is unavoidable in his culture. The neurotic person, on the other hand, suffers invariably more than the average person. He invariably has to pay an exorbitant price for his defenses, consisting in an impairment in vitality and expansiveness, or more specifically in an impairment of his capacities for achievement and enjoyment, resulting in the discrepancy I have mentioned. In fact, the neurotic is invariably a suffering person. The only reason why I did not mention this fact when discussing the characteristics of all neuroses that can be derived from surface observation is that it is not necessarily observable from without. The neurotic himself may not even be aware of the fact that he is suffering.

Talking of fears and defenses, I am afraid that by this time many readers will have become impatient about such an extensive discussion of so simple a question as what constitutes a neurosis. In defending myself I may point out that psychic phenomena are always intricate, that while there are seemingly simple questions there is never a simple answer, that the predicament we meet here at the beginning is no exceptional one, but will accompany us throughout the book, whatever problem we shall tackle. The particular difficulty in the description of a neurosis lies in the fact that a satisfactory answer can be given neither with psychological nor with sociological tools alone, but that they must be taken up alternately, first one and then the other, as in fact we have done. If we should regard a neurosis only from the point of view of its dynamics and psychic structure we should hypostatize a normal human being: he does not exist. We run into more difficulties as soon as we pass the borderline of our own country or of countries with a culture similar to our own. And if we regard a neurosis only from the sociological point of view as a mere deviation from the behavior pattern common to a certain society, we neglect grossly all we know about the psychological characteristics of a neurosis, and no psychiatrist of any school or country would recognize the results as what he is accustomed to designate a neurosis. The reconcilement of the two approaches lies in a method of observation that considers the deviation both in the manifest picture of the neurosis and in the dynamics of the psychic processes, but without considering either deviation as the primary and decisive one. The two must be combined. This in general is the way we have gone in pointing out that fear and defense are one of the dynamic centers of a neurosis, but constitute a neurosis only when deviating in quantity or quality from the fears and defenses patterned in the same culture.

We have to go one step farther in the same direction. There is still another essential characteristic of a neurosis and that is the presence of conflicting tendencies of the existence of which, or at least of the precise content of which, the neurotic himself is unaware, and for which he automatically tries to reach certain compromise solutions. It is this latter characteristic which in various forms Freud has stressed as an indispensable constituent of neuroses. What distinguishes the neurotic conflicts from those commonly existing in a culture is neither their content nor the fact that they are essentially unconscious—in both respects the common cultural conflicts may be identical—but the fact that in the neurotic the conflicts are sharper and more accentuated. The neurotic person attempts and arrives at compromise solutions—not inopportunely classified as neurotic—and these solutions are less satisfactory than those of the average individual and are achieved at great expense to the whole personality.

Reviewing all these considerations, we are not yet able to give a well-rounded definition of a neurosis, but we can arrive at a description: a neurosis is a psychic disturbance brought about by fears and defenses against these fears, and by attempts to find compromise solutions for conflicting tendencies. For practical reasons it is advisable to call this disturbance a neurosis only if it deviates from the pattern common to the particular culture.

· CHAPTER 2 ·

Reasons for Speaking of a "Neurotic Personality of Our Time"

SINCE our interest is focussed on the ways in which a neurosis affects the personality, the scope of our inquiry is limited in two directions. In the first place, there are neuroses which may occur in individuals whose personality is otherwise intact and undistorted, developing as a reaction to an external situation which is filled with conflicts. After discussing the nature of certain basic psychic processes we shall come back and consider briefly the structure of these simple situation neuroses.[1] We are not primarily interested in them here, because they reveal no neurotic personality but only a momentary lack of adaptation to a given difficult situation. When speaking of neuroses I shall refer to character neuroses, that is, conditions in which—though the symptomatic picture may be exactly like that of a situation neurosis—the main disturbance lies in the deformations of the character.[2] They are the result of an insidious chronic process, starting as a rule in childhood and involving greater or lesser parts of the personality in a greater or lesser intensity. Seen from the surface a character neurosis, too, may result from an

[1] The situation neuroses coincide roughly with what J. H. Schultz has called *Exogene Fremdneurosen*.

[2] Franz Alexander has suggested the term character neuroses for those neuroses lacking clinical symptoms. I do not think this term is tenable because the absence or presence of symptoms is often irrelevant for the nature of a neurosis.

actual situation conflict, but a carefully collected history of the person may show that difficult character traits were present long before any confusing situation arose, that the momentary predicament is itself to a large extent due to previously existing personal difficulties, and furthermore that the person reacts neurotically to a life situation which for the average healthy individual does not imply any conflict at all. The situation merely reveals the presence of a neurosis which may have existed for some time.

In the second place, we are not so much interested in the symptomatic picture of the neurosis. Our interest lies predominantly in the character disturbances themselves, because deformations of the personality are the ever-recurring picture in neuroses, whereas symptoms in the clinical sense may vary or be entirely lacking. Also from a cultural viewpoint character formation is more important than symptoms, because it is character, not symptoms, that influences human behavior. With greater knowledge of the structure of neuroses and with the realization that the cure of a symptom does not necessarily mean the cure of a neurosis, psychoanalysts in general have shifted their interest and given more attention to character deformations than to symptoms. Speaking figuratively we may say that the neurotic symptoms are not the volcano itself but rather its eruptions, while the pathogenic conflict, like the volcano, is hidden deep down in the individual, unknown to himself.

These restrictions granted we may raise the question whether neurotic persons today have traits in common which are so essential that we may speak of a neurotic personality of our time.

As to the character deformations which accompany different types of neuroses, we are struck by their differences rather than by their similarities. The hysterical character, for instance, is decidedly different from the compulsive character. The differences which strike our attention, however, are differences of mechanisms or, in more general terms, differences in the ways the two disturbances manifest themselves and in the ways in which they are solved, such as the great role of projection in the hysterical type as compared with the intellectualization of conflicts in the compulsive type. On the other hand, the similarities which I have in mind do not concern the manifestations or the ways in which they have been brought about, but they concern the content of the conflict itself. To be more exact, the similarities are not so much in the experiences which have genetically prompted the disturbance but in the conflicts which are actually moving the person.

To elucidate the motivating forces and their ramifications one presupposition is necessary. Freud and the majority of the analysts put their main emphasis on the principle that the task of analyzing is fulfilled by discovering either the sexual roots (for instance the specific erogenic zones) of an impulse or the infantile pattern of which it is supposed to be a repetition. Though I hold that a complete understanding of a neurosis is not possible without tracing it back to its infantile conditions, I believe that the genetic approach, if used onesidedly, confuses rather than clarifies the issue, because it leads then to a neglect of the actually existing unconscious tendencies and their functions and interactions with other tendencies that are present, such as impulses, fears and protective measures. Genetic understanding is useful only as long as it helps the functional understanding.

Proceeding on this belief I have found in analyzing the most varied kinds of personalities, belonging to different types of neuroses, differing in age, temperament and interests, coming from different social layers, that the contents of the dynamically central conflicts and their interrelations were essentially similar in all of them.[3] My experiences in psychoanalytical practice have been confirmed by observations of persons outside the practice and of characters in current literature. If the recurring problems of neurotic persons are divested of the fantastic and abstruse character they often have, it cannot escape our attention that they differ only in quantity from the problems bothering the normal person in our culture. The great majority of us have to struggle with problems of competition, fears of failure, emotional isolation, distrust of others and of our own selves, to mention only a few of the problems that may be present in a neurosis.

The fact that in general the majority of individuals in a culture have to face the same problems suggests the conclusion that these problems have been created by the specific life conditions existing in that culture. That they do not represent problems common to "human nature" seems to be warranted by the fact that the motivating forces and conflicts in other cultures are different from ours.

Hence in speaking of a neurotic personality of our time, I not only mean that there are neurotic persons

[3] Emphasis on the similarities does not at all mean a disregard for the scientific efforts made to elaborate special types of neuroses. On the contrary, I am fully convinced that psychopathology has achieved notable progress in delineating circumscribed pictures of psychic disturbances, their genesis, their special structure, their peculiar manifestations.

having essential peculiarities in common, but also that these basic similarities are essentially produced by the difficulties existing in our time and culture. As far as my sociological knowledge allows me I shall show later on what difficulties of our culture are responsible for the psychic conflicts we have.

The validity of my assumption concerning the relation between culture and neurosis ought to be tested by the combined efforts of anthropologists and psychiatrists. The psychiatrists would not only have to study neuroses as they appear in definite cultures, as has been done from formal criteria such as frequency, severity or type of neuroses, but particularly they should study them from the point of view of what basic conflicts are underlying them. The anthropologists would have to study the same culture from the point of view of what psychic difficulties its structure creates for the individual. One way in which the similarity in basic conflicts expresses itself is a similarity of attitudes open to surface observation. By surface observation I mean what a good observer can discover without the tools of psychoanalytic technique, concerning persons with whom he is thoroughly familiar, such as himself, his friends, members of his family or his colleagues. I shall start with a short cross-section of such possible frequent observations.

The attitudes thus observable may be loosely classified as follows: first, attitudes concerning giving and getting affections; second, attitudes concerning evaluation of the self; third, attitudes concerning self-assertion; fourth, aggression; fifth, sexuality.

As to the first, one of the predominant trends of neurotics of our time is their excessive dependence on the

approval or affection of others. We all want to be liked
and to feel appreciated, but in neurotic persons the dependence on affection or approval is disproportionate
to the real significance which other persons have for
their lives. Although we all wish to be liked by persons
of whom we are fond, in neurotics there is an indiscriminate hunger for appreciation or affection, regardless of whether they care for the person concerned or
whether the judgment of that person has any meaning
for them. More often than not they are not aware of
this boundless craving, but they betray its existence in
their sensitivity when the attention they want is not
forthcoming. They may feel hurt, for example, if someone does not accept their invitation, does not telephone
for some time, or even only if he disagrees with them in
some opinion. This sensitivity may be concealed by a
"don't care" attitude.

Furthermore, there is a marked contradiction between their wish for affection and their own capacity
for feeling or giving it. Excessive demands concerning
consideration for their own wishes may go with just as
great a lack of consideration for others. The contradiction does not always appear on the surface. The neurotic may, for example, be overconsiderate and eager to
be helpful to everyone, but if this is the case it is notice-
able that he acts compulsively, not out of a spontaneously radiating warmth.

The inner insecurity expressed in this dependence on
others is the second feature that strikes us in neurotics
on surface observation. Feelings of inferiority and inadequacy are characteristics that never fail. They may
appear in a number of ways—such as a conviction of
incompetence, of stupidity, of unattractiveness—and

they may exist without any basis in reality. Notions of
their own stupidity may be found in persons who are
unusually intelligent, or notions about their own unattractiveness in the most beautiful women. These feelings of inferiority may appear openly on the surface in
the form of complaints or worries, or the alleged defects
may be taken for granted as a fact on which it is super-
fluous to waste any thought. On the other hand, they
may be covered up by compensating needs for self-
aggrandizement, by a compulsive propensity to show
off, to impress others and one's self with all sorts of at-
tributes that lend prestige in our culture, such as money,
possession of old pictures, old furniture, women, social
contacts with prominent people, travel, or superior
knowledge. One or the other of these tendencies may be
entirely in the foreground, but more generally one will
feel distinctly the presence of both tendencies.

The third set of attitudes, those concerning self-
assertion, involve definite inhibitions. By self-assertion
I mean the act of asserting one's self or one's claims,
and I use it without any connotation of undue pushing
forward. In this respect neurotics reveal a comprehensive group of inhibitions. They have inhibitions about
expressing their wishes or asking for something, about
doing something in their own interest, expressing an
opinion or warranted criticism, ordering someone, se-
lecting the people they wish to associate with, making
contacts with people, and so on. There are inhibitions
also in reference to what we might describe as maintaining one's stand: neurotics often are incapable of defending themselves against attack, or of saying "no" if
they do not wish to comply with the wishes of others, as
for example to a saleswoman who wants to sell them

something they do not want to buy, or to a person who invites them to a party, or to a woman or man who wants to make love. There are finally the inhibitions toward knowing what they want: difficulties in making decisions, forming opinions, daring to express wishes which concern only their own benefit. Such wishes have to be concealed: a friend of mine in her personal accounts puts "movies" under "education" and "liquors" under "health." Particularly important in this latter group is the incapacity to plan,[4] whether it be a trip or a plan of life: neurotics let themselves drift, even in important decisions such as a profession or marriage, instead of having clear conceptions of what they want in life. They are driven exclusively by certain neurotic fears, as we see in persons who pile up money because they fear impoverishment, or take part in endless love affairs because they fear to enter a constructive piece of work.

By the fourth set of difficulties, those concerning aggression, I mean, in contradistinction to the attitudes of self-assertion, acts of going against someone, attacking, disparaging, encroaching, or any form of hostile behavior. Disturbances of this kind show themselves in two entirely different ways. One way is a propensity to be aggressive, domineering, over-exacting, to boss, cheat or find fault. Occasionally persons who have these attitudes are aware of being aggressive; more often they are not in the least aware of it and are convinced subjectively that they are just being honest or merely expressing an opinion, or even being modest in their demands, although in reality they are offensive and

4 Schultz-Hencke in *Schicksal und Neurose* is one of the few psycho-analytic writers who has paid adequate attention to this important point.

imposing. In others, however, these disturbances show themselves in the opposite way. One finds on the surface an attitude of easily feeling cheated, dominated, scolded, imposed on or humiliated. These persons, too, are frequently not aware that this is only their own attitude, but believe sadly that the whole world is down on them, imposing on them.

Peculiarities of the fifth kind, those in the sexual sphere, may be classified roughly as either a compulsive need for sexual activities or inhibitions toward such activities. Inhibitions may appear at any step leading to sexual satisfaction. They may set in at the approach of persons of the other sex, in wooing, in the sexual functions themselves or in the enjoyment. All the peculiarities described in the preceding groups will appear also in the sexual attitudes.

One might go to much greater length in describing the attitudes I have mentioned. I shall have to come back to each of them later, however, and a more exhaustive description now would add little to our understanding. In order to understand them better we shall have to consider the dynamic processes which bring them about. Knowing the underlying dynamic processes we shall see that all of these attitudes, incoherent as they may seem, are structurally interrelated.

· CHAPTER 3 ·

Anxiety

BEFORE going into a more detailed discussion of present-day neuroses I have to pick up one of the loose ends I left in the first chapter and clarify what I mean by anxiety. It is important to do this because, as I have said, anxiety is the dynamic center of neuroses and thus we shall have to deal with it all the time.

I used the term before as synonymous with fear, thereby indicating a kinship between the two. Both are in fact emotional reactions to danger and both may be accompanied by physical sensations, such as trembling, perspiration, violent heart-beat, which may be so strong that a sudden, intense fear may lead to death. Yet there is a difference between the two.

When a mother is afraid that her child will die when it has only a pimple or a slight cold we speak of anxiety; but if she is afraid when the child has a serious illness we call her reaction fear. If someone is afraid whenever he stands on a height or when he has to discuss a topic he knows well, we call his reaction anxiety; if someone is afraid when he loses his way high up in the mountains during a heavy thunderstorm we would speak of fear. Thus far we should have a simple and neat distinction: fear is a reaction that is proportionate to the danger one has to face, whereas anxiety is a disproportionate reaction to danger, or even a reaction to imaginary danger.[1]

This distinction has one flaw, however, which is that the decision as to whether the reaction is proportionate depends on the average knowledge existing in the particular culture. But even if that knowledge proclaims a certain attitude to be unfounded, a neurotic will find no difficulty in giving nis action a rational foundation. In fact, one might get into hopeless arguments if one told a patient that his dread of being attacked by some raving lunatic is neurotic anxiety. He would point out that his fear is realistic and would refer to occurrences of the kind he fears. The primitive would be similarly stubborn if one considered certain of his fear reactions disproportionate to the actual danger. For instance, a primitive man in a tribe which has taboos on eating certain animals is mortally frightened if by any chance he has eaten the tabooed meat. As an outside observer you would call this a disproportionate reaction, in fact an entirely unwarranted one. But knowing the tribe's beliefs concerning forbidden meat you would have to realize that the situation represents a real danger to the man, danger that the hunting or fishing grounds may be spoiled or danger of contracting an illness.

There is a difference, however, between the anxiety we find in primitives and the anxiety we consider neurotic in our culture. The content of neurotic anxiety, unlike that of the primitive, does not conform with commonly held opinions. In both the impression of a dis-

[1] Freud in his *New Introductory Lectures*, chapter on "Anxiety and Instinctual Life," makes a similar distinction between "objective" and "neurotic" anxiety, describing the former as an "intelligible reaction to danger."

proportionate reaction vanishes once the meaning of
the anxiety is understood. There are persons, for example, who have a perpetual anxiety about dying; on
the other hand, because of their sufferings they have a
secret wish to die. Their various fears of death, combined with their wishful thinking with regard to death,
create a strong apprehension of imminent danger. If
one knows all these factors one cannot help but call
their anxiety about dying an adequate reaction. Another, simplified example is seen in persons who become terrified when they find themselves near a preci-
pice or a high window or on a high bridge. Here again,
from without, the fear reaction seems to be disproportionate. But such a situation may present to them, or
stir up in them, a conflict between the wish to live and
the temptation for some reason or another to jump
down from the heights. It is this conflict that may result
in anxiety.

All these considerations suggest a change in the definition. Fear and anxiety are both proportionate reactions to danger, but in the case of fear the danger is a
transparent, objective one and in the case of anxiety it
is hidden and subjective. That is, the intensity of the
anxiety is proportionate to the meaning the situation
has for the person concerned, and the reasons why he is
thus anxious are essentially unknown to him.

The practical implication of the distinction between
fear and anxiety is that the attempt to argue a neurotic
out of his anxiety—the method of persuasion—is useless. His anxiety concerns not the situation as it stands
actually in reality, but the situation as it appears to
him. The therapeutic task, therefore, can be only that
of finding out the meaning certain situations have for
him.

Having qualified what we mean by anxiety we have to get an idea of the role it plays. The average person in our culture is little aware of the importance anxiety has in his life. Usually he remembers only that he had some anxiety in his childhood, that he had one or more anxiety dreams, and that he was inordinately apprehensive in a situation outside his daily routine, as, for instance, before an important talk with an influential person or before examinations.

The information we get from neurotic persons on this score is anything but uniform. Some neurotics are fully aware of being hounded by anxiety. Its manifestations vary immensely: it may appear as diffused anxiety, in the form of anxiety-attacks; it may be attached to definite situations or activities, such as heights, streets, public performances; it may have a definite content, such as apprehension about becoming insane, getting cancer, swallowing pins. Others realize that they have anxiety now and then, with or without knowing the conditions that provoke it, but they do not attribute any importance to it. Finally there are neurotic persons who are aware only of having depressions, feelings of inadequacy, disturbances in sex life, and the like, but they are entirely unaware of ever having or having had anxiety. Closer investigation, however, usually proves their first statement to be inaccurate. In analyzing these persons one invariably finds just as much anxiety beneath the surface as in the first group, if not more. The analysis makes these neurotic persons conscious of their previous anxiety and they may recall anxiety dreams or situations in which they felt apprehensive. Yet the extent of anxiety acknowledged by them usually does not surpass the normal. This suggests that we may have anxiety without knowing it.

When it is put in this way the significance of the problem involved here does not show. It is part of a more comprehensive problem. We have feelings of affection, anger, suspicion, so fleeting that they scarcely invade awareness, and so transitory that we forget them. These feelings may really be irrelevant and transitory; but they may just as well have behind them a great dynamic force. The degree of awareness of a feeling does not indicate anything of its strength or importance.[2] Concerning anxiety this means not only that we may have anxiety without knowing it, but that anxiety may be the determining factor in our lives without our being conscious of it.

In fact, we seem to go to any length to escape anxiety or to avoid feeling it. There are many reasons for this, the most general reason being that intense anxiety is one of the most tormenting affects we can have. Patients who have gone through an intense fit of anxiety will tell you that they would rather die than have a recurrence of that experience. Besides, certain elements contained in the affect of anxiety may be particularly unbearable for the individual. One of them is helplessness. One can be active and courageous in the face of a great danger. But in a state of anxiety one feels—in fact, is—helpless. To be rendered helpless is particularly unbearable for those persons for whom power, ascendancy, the idea of being master of any situation, is a prevailing ideal. Impressed by the apparent disproportion of their reaction they resent it, as if it demonstrated a weakness or a cowardice.

Another element in anxiety is its apparent irration-

---

[2] This is merely a paraphrase of one aspect of Freud's basic discovery of the importance of unconscious factors.

ality. To allow any irrational factors to control them is for some persons more intolerable than for others. It is particularly hard to endure for those who secretly feel in danger of being swamped by irrational contrasting forces within themselves, and who have automatically trained themselves to exercise a strict intellectual control. Thus they will not consciously tolerate any irrational elements. Besides containing individual motivations this latter reaction involves a cultural factor, inasmuch as our culture places great stress on rational thinking and behavior and regards irrationality, or what may appear as such, as inferior.

To a certain extent connected with this is the last element in anxiety: by its very irrationality anxiety presents an implicit admonition that something within us is out of gear, and therefore it is a challenge to overhaul something within ourselves. Not that we consciously take it as a challenge; but implicitly it is one, whether we choose to acknowledge it or not. None of us likes such a challenge; it may be said that we are opposed to nothing so much as to the realization that we must change some attitude of our own. The more hopelessly, however, a person feels trapped in the intricate network of his fear and defense mechanism, and the more he has to cling to his delusion that he is right and perfect in everything, the more he instinctively rejects any—even if it is only indirect or implicit—insinuation of something wrong in himself and any need to change.

In our culture there are four main ways of escaping anxiety: rationalize it; deny it; narcotize it; avoid thoughts, feelings, impulses and situations which might arouse it.

The first method—rationalization—is the best explanation for evasion of responsibility: It consists in turning anxiety into a rational fear. If the psychic value of such a shift is disregarded we might imagine that not much is changed by it. The over-solicitous mother is in fact just as concerned about her children, regardless of whether she admits to having anxiety or whether she interprets her anxiety as a justified fear. One can any number of times, however, make the experiment of telling such a mother that her reaction is not a rational fear but an anxiety, implying that it is disproportionate to the existing danger and involves personal factors. In response she will refute this insinuation and will put all her energy into proving you entirely wrong. Did Mary not catch this infectious disease in the nursery? Did Johnny not break his leg climbing trees? Has not a man tried recently to lure children by promising them candy? Is her own behavior not entirely dictated by affection and duty?[3]

Whenever we meet such a vigorous defense of irrational attitudes we may be sure that the attitude defended has important functions for the individual. Instead of feeling a helpless prey to her emotions, such a mother feels she can actively do something about the situation. Instead of recognizing a weakness she can feel proud of her high standards. Instead of admitting that irrational elements pervade her attitude she feels entirely rational and justified. Instead of seeing and accepting a challenge to change something within herself she can go on shifting the responsibility to the outside world and thereby escape facing her own motivations. Of course she has to pay the price for these momentary advantages by never getting rid of her wor-

[3] *Cf.* Sandor Rado, *An Over-Solicitous Mother.*

ries. Particularly do the children have to pay the price. But she does not realize that, and in the last analysis she does not want to realize it, because deep down she clings to the delusion that she can change nothing within herself and yet manage to have all the benefits that would ensue from a change.

The same principle holds true for all tendencies to believe that anxiety is a rational fear, whatever its content may be: fear of childbirth, of diseases, of errors in diet, of catastrophes, of impoverishment.

The second way of escaping anxiety is to deny its existence. In fact, nothing is done about anxiety in such cases *except* denying it, that is, excluding it from consciousness. All that appears are the physical concomitants of fear or anxiety, such as shivering, sweating, accelerated heart-beat, choking sensations, frequent urge to urinate, diarrhea, vomiting, and, in the mental sphere, a feeling of restlessness, of being rushed or paralyzed. We may have all these feelings and physical sensations when we are afraid and are aware of being so; they may also be the exclusive expression of an existing anxiety which is suppressed. In the latter case all that the individual knows about his condition is such outward evidence as the fact that he has to urinate frequently in certain conditions, that he becomes nauseated on trains, that at times he has night-sweats, and always without any physical cause.

It is also possible, however, to make a conscious denial of anxiety, a conscious attempt to overcome it. This is akin to what happens on the normal level, when it is attempted to get rid of fear by recklessly disregarding it. The most familiar example on the normal level is the soldier who, driven by the impulse to overcome a fear, performs heroic deeds.

The neurotic, too, may make a conscious decision to overcome his anxiety. A girl, for example, who was tormented by anxiety until close to puberty, particularly concerning burglars, consciously decided to disregard the anxiety, to sleep alone in the attic, to walk alone in the empty house. The first dream she brought to analysis revealed several variations of this attitude. It contained several situations which in fact were frightening, but which each time she faced with bravery. In one of them she heard footsteps in the garden at night, stepped out on the balcony and called "Who's there?" She succeeded in losing her fear of burglars, but as nothing was changed in the factors provoking her anxiety, other consequences of the still-existing anxiety remained. She continued to be withdrawn and timid, she felt unwanted and could not settle down to any constructive work.

Very often there is no such conscious decision in neurotics. Frequently the process goes on automatically. The difference from the normal, however, does not lie in the degree of consciousness of the decision, but in the result attained. All that a neurotic can attain by "pulling himself together" is to lose a special manifestation of anxiety, as the girl lost her fear concerning burglars. I do not mean to undervaluate such a result. It may have a practical value and may also have a psychic value in strengthening self-esteem. But since such results are usually over-estimated it is necessary to point out the negative side.[4] Not only does the essential dynamics of the personality remain unchanged, but when the neurotic loses a conspicuous manifestation of his existing

---

[4] Freud has always stressed this point in emphasizing that the disappearance of symptoms is not a sufficient indication of cure.

disturbances he loses at the same time a vital stimulus to tackle them.

The process of ruthlessly marching over an anxiety plays a great role in many neuroses and is not always recognized for what it is. The aggressiveness, for instance, which many neurotics display in certain situations is often taken as a direct expression of an actual hostility, while it may be primarily such a reckless marching over an existing timidity, under the pressure of feeling attacked. While some hostility is usually present, the neurotic may greatly overdo the aggression he really feels, his anxiety provoking him to overcome his timidity. If this is overlooked there is danger of mistaking recklessness for veritable aggression.

The third way of finding release from anxiety is to narcotize it. This may be done consciously and literally by taking to alcohol or drugs. There are, however, many ways of doing it, without the connection being obvious. One of them is to plunge into social activities because of fear of being alone; it does not alter the situation whether this fear is recognized as such or appears only as a vague uneasiness. Another way of narcotizing anxiety is to drown it in work, a procedure to be recognized from the compulsive character of the work and from the uneasiness that appears on Sundays and holidays. The same end may be served by an inordinate need for sleep, although usually not much refreshment results from the sleep. Finally, sexual activities may serve as the safety-valve through which anxiety can be released. It has long been known that compulsive masturbation may be provoked by anxiety, but the same holds true for all sorts of sexual relations. Persons for whom sexual activities serve predominantly as a means of allaying anxiety will become extremely restless and irritable if they have no chance for sexual satisfaction, if even for a short time.

The fourth way of escaping anxiety is the most radical: it consists in avoiding all situations, thoughts or feelings which might arouse anxiety. This may be a conscious process, as when the person who fears diving or mountain climbing avoids doing these things. More accurately speaking, a person may be aware of the existence of anxiety and aware of avoiding it. He may also, however, be only dimly or not at all aware of having anxiety, and dimly or not at all aware of avoiding activities. He may, for instance, procrastinate in matters which, without his knowledge, are connected with anxiety, such as making decisions, going to the doctor or writing a letter. Or he may "pretend," that is, subjectively believe that certain activities he contemplates —such as taking part in a discussion, giving orders to employees, separating himself from another person— are unimportant. Or he may "pretend" not to like doing certain things and discard them on that basis. Thus a girl to whom going to parties involves fears of being neglected may avoid going altogether by making herself believe that she does not like social gatherings.

If we go one step farther, to the point where such avoidance operates automatically, we have the phenomenon of an inhibition. An inhibition consists in an inability to do, feel or think certain things, and its function is to avoid the anxiety which would arise if the person attempted to do, feel or think those things. There is no anxiety present in awareness, and no capacity for overcoming the inhibition by conscious effort. Inhibitions are present in their most spectacular form in the hysterical losses of functioning: hysterical blindness, speechlessness or paralysis of a limb. In the sexual sphere frigidity and impotence represent such inhibitions, although the structure of these sexual inhibitions may be very complex. In the mental sphere inhibitions in concentration, in forming or expressing opinions, in making contacts with people are well-known phenomena.

It might be worth while to spend several pages merely enumerating inhibitions, so as to convey a full impression of the variety of their forms and the frequency of their occurrence. I think, however, that I may leave it to the reader to review his own observations on that score, because inhibitions are nowadays a well-known phenomenon and easily recognizable, if they are fully developed. Nevertheless it is desirable to consider briefly the preconditions that are necessary in order to become aware that inhibitions exist. Otherwise we should underestimate their frequency because usually we are not aware of how many inhibitions we really have.

In the first place, we must be aware of the desire to do something in order to be aware of the inability to do it. For instance, we have to be aware of possessing ambitions before we can realize that we have inhibitions on that score. The question may be asked whether we do not always at least know what we want. Decidedly not. Let us consider, for example, a person listening to a paper and having critical thoughts about it. A minor inhibition would consist in a timidity about expressing the criticism; a stronger inhibition would prevent him from organizing his thoughts, with the result that they would occur to him only after the discussion was over, or the next morning. But the inhibition may go so far as not to permit the critical thoughts to come up at all, and in this case, assuming that he really feels critical, he will be inclined to accept blindly what has been said or even to admire it; and he will be quite unaware of having any inhibitions. In other words, if an inhibition goes so far as to check wishes or impulses there can be no awareness of its existence.

A second factor that may prevent awareness occurs when an inhibition has such an important function in a person's life that he prefers to insist that it is an unchangeable fact. If, for instance, there is an overpowering anxiety of some kind connected with any sort of competitive work, resulting in an intense fatigue after every attempt to work, the person may insist that he is not strong enough to do any work; that belief protects him, but if he admitted an inhibition he might have to return to work and thereby expose himself to the dreaded anxiety.

A third possibility brings us back to the cultural factors. It may be impossible ever to become aware of personal inhibitions if they coincide with culturally approved forms of inhibitions or with existing ideologies. A patient who had serious inhibitions against approaching women was not aware of being inhibited because he saw his conduct in the light of the accepted idea of the sacredness of women. An inhibition against making demands is easily put on the basis of the dogma that modesty is a virtue; an inhibition against critical thinking about dogmas dominant in politics or religion or any specific field of interest may escape attention, and we may be entirely unaware of the existence of an anxiety concerning exposure to punishment, criticism or isolation. In order to judge the situation, however, we must

of course know the individual factors in great detail.
The absence of critical thought does not necessarily imply the existence of inhibitions, but may be due to a
general laziness of mind, to stupidity or to conviction
that really coincides with the dominant dogma.

Any of these three factors may account for the inability to recognize existing inhibitions and for the fact
that even experienced psychoanalysts may find it difficult to detect them. But even assuming that we could
recognize all of them, our estimate of the frequency of
inhibitions would still be too low. We would have to take
into account all those reactions which, although not
fully grown inhibitions, are on the way toward that cul-
mination. In the attitudes I have in mind we are still
able to do certain things, but the anxiety connected with
them exerts certain influences on the activities themselves.

In the first place, undertaking an activity about which
we feel anxiety produces a feeling of strain, fatigue or
exhaustion. One patient of mine, for example, who was
recovering from a fear of walking on the street but still
had a good deal of anxiety on that score, felt completely
exhausted when she took a walk on Sundays. That this
exhaustion was not due to any physical weakness is
shown by the fact that she could perform strenuous
housework without the slightest fatigue. It was the
anxiety bound up with walking outdoors that caused the
exhaustion; the anxiety was diminished enough so that
she could walk outdoors, but was still effective enough
to exhaust her. Many difficulties commonly ascribed to
overwork are in reality caused not by the work itself
but by anxiety about the work or about relations with
colleagues.

In the second place, anxiety connected with a certain

activity will result in an impairment of that function. If there is, for example, an anxiety connected with giving orders, they will be given in an apologetic, ineffectual manner. Anxiety about riding a horse will result in an inability to master the animal. The degree of awareness varies. A person may be aware that anxiety prevents him from performing tasks in a satisfactory way, or he may only have the feeling that he is unable to do anything well.

Thirdly, anxiety connected with an activity will spoil the pleasure that it would otherwise hold. This is not true for minor anxieties; on the contrary, they may produce an added zest. Riding a roller-coaster with some apprehension may make it more thrilling, whereas doing it with strong anxiety will make it a torture. A strong anxiety connected with sexual relations will render them thoroughly unenjoyable, and if one is not aware of the anxiety one will have the feeling that sexual relations do not mean anything.

This last point may be confusing, because I have said above that a feeling of dislike may be used as a means of avoiding an anxiety, and now I am saying that the dislike may be a consequence of the anxiety. Actually, both statements are true. Dislike may be the means of avoiding and the consequence of having anxiety. This is one small example of the difficulty in understanding psychic phenomena. They are intricate and involved, and unless we make up our minds that we must consider innumerable, interwoven interactions we shall make no progress in psychological knowledge.

The purpose of discussing how we may defend ourselves against anxiety is not to give an exhaustive picture of all possible defenses. In fact we shall soon learn more radical ways of preventing anxiety from arising. My main concern now is to substantiate the statement that one may have more anxiety than one is aware of, or may have anxiety without being aware of it at all, and also to show some of the more common points where it may be looked for.

Thus, in short, anxiety may be hidden behind feelings of physical discomfort, such as heart-pounding and fatigue; it may be concealed by a number of fears that seem rational or warranted; it may be the hidden force driving us to drink or to submerge ourselves in all sorts of distractions. We shall often find it as the cause of inability to do or enjoy certain things, and we shall always discover it as the promoting factor behind inhibitions.

For reasons we shall discuss later, our culture generates a great deal of anxiety in the individuals living in it. Hence practically everyone has built up one or another of the defenses I have mentioned. The more neurotic a person is, the more is his personality pervaded and determined by such defenses, and the greater the number of things he is unable to do or does not consider doing, although according to his vitality, mental capacities or educational background one would be justified in expecting him to do them. The more severe the neurosis, the more inhibitions are present, both subtle and gross.[5]

---

[5] H. Schultz-Hencke in *Einfuehrung in die Psychoanalyse* has particularly emphasized the paramount importance of the *Luecken*, that is, the gaps which we find in the life and personality of neurotics.

CHAPTER 4

Anxiety and Hostility

WHEN discussing the difference between fear and anxiety we found as our first result that anxiety is a fear which essentially involves a subjective factor. What then is the nature of this subjective factor?

Let us start by describing the experience an individual undergoes during anxiety. He has the feeling of a powerful, inescapable danger against which he himself is entirely helpless. Whatever the manifestations of anxiety, whether it be a hypochondriac fear of cancer, anxiety concerning thunderstorms, a phobia about high places, or any comparable fear, the two factors of an overpowering danger and defenselessness against it are invariably present. Sometimes the dangerous force against which he feels helpless may be felt to come from outside—thunderstorms, cancer, accidents and the like; sometimes the danger is felt to threaten him from his own ungovernable impulses—fear of having to jump down from a high place, or to cut someone with a knife; sometimes the danger is entirely vague and intangible, as it often is in an anxiety attack.

Such feelings in themselves, however, are not characteristic only of anxiety; they may be exactly the same in any situation which involves a factual overpowering danger and a factual helplessness toward it. I imagine that the subjective experience of persons during an earthquake, or of an infant under two years of age exposed to brutalities, is in no way different from the subjective experience of one who has anxiety concerning thunderstorms. In the case of fear the danger is present in reality and the feeling of helplessness is conditioned by reality, and in the case of anxiety the danger is generated or magnified by intrapsychic factors and the helplessness is conditioned by one's own attitude.

The question concerning the subjective factor in anxiety is thus reduced to the more specific inquiry: what are the psychic conditions that create the feeling of an imminent powerful danger and an attitude of helplessness toward it? This at any rate is the question that the psychologist has to raise. That chemical conditions in the body can also create the feeling and the physical concomitants of anxiety is as little a psychological problem as the fact that chemical conditions can produce elation or sleep.

In tackling this problem of anxiety Freud has, as so often in other problems, shown us the direction in which to move. He has done this by his crucial discovery that the subjective factor involved in anxiety lies in our own instinctual drives; in other words, both the danger anticipated by anxiety and the feeling of helplessness toward it are conjured by the explosive force of our own impulses. I shall discuss Freud's views in more detail at the end of this chapter, and shall also point out in what way my conclusions differ from his.

In principle, any impulse has the potential power to provoke anxiety, provided that its discovery or pursuit would mean a violation of other vital interests or needs, and provided that it is sufficiently imperative or passionate. In periods when there are definite and severe sexual taboos, like the Victorian era, yielding to sexual impulses has often meant incurring a realistic danger. An unmarried girl, for example, had to face a real danger of tortured conscience or social disgrace, and those yielding to masturbating urges had to face a real danger in so far as they were subject to threats of castration or warnings of fatal physical injuries or mental diseases. The same holds true today for certain perverted sex impulses, such as exhibitionistic drives or impulses directed toward children. In our times, however, as far as "normal" sex impulses are concerned, our attitude has become so lenient that admitting them to ourselves, or carrying them out in reality, involves serious danger much less frequently; hence there is less factual reason for apprehension on that score.

The change in the cultural attitude toward sex may be greatly responsible for the fact that, according to my experience, sexual impulses as such are only in exceptional cases found to be the dynamic force behind anxiety. This statement may seem exaggerated, because no doubt on the surface anxiety does seem to be linked with sexual desires. Neurotic persons are often found to have anxiety in connection with sexual intercourse, or to have inhibitions on that score as a consequence of anxiety. Closer analysis shows, however, that the basis of anxiety usually lies not in the sex impulses as such but in hostile impulses coupled with them, such as the impulse to hurt or humiliate the partner through intercourse.

In fact, *hostile impulses of various kinds form the main source from which neurotic anxiety springs.* I am afraid lest this new statement should sound again like an unjustified generalization from what may be true for some cases. But these cases, in which one can find a direct connection between the hostility and the anxiety it promotes, are not the only basis for my statement. It is well known that an acute hostile impulse may be the direct cause of anxiety, if its pursuit would mean defeating the purposes of the self. One example may serve for many. F. goes on a hiking trip through the mountains with a girl, Mary, to whom he is deeply devoted. Nevertheless he feels acutely and savagely infuriated against her because his jealousy has somehow been aroused. When walking with her on a precipitous mountain path he gets a severe attack of anxiety, with heavy breathing and heart-pounding, because of a conscious impulse to push the girl over the edge of the path. The structure of anxieties like these is the same as indicated in anxieties from sexual sources: an imperative impulse which, if yielded to, would mean a catastrophe for the self.

In the great majority of persons, however, a direct causal connection between hostility and neurotic anxiety is far from evident. In order, then, to make it clear why I declare that in the neuroses of our time hostile impulses are the main psychological force promoting anxiety, it is necessary to examine now in some detail the psychological consequences which result from a repression of hostility.

Repressing a hostility means "pretending" that everything is all right and thus refraining from fighting when we ought to fight, or at least when we wish to fight. Hence the first unavoidable consequence of such a repression is that it generates a feeling of defenselessness, or to be more exact, it reinforces an already given feeling of defenselessness. If hostility is repressed when a person's interests are factually attacked it becomes possible for others to take advantage of him.

The experience of a chemist, C., represents an every-

day occurrence of this kind. C. had what was regarded
as nervous exhaustion as a consequence of too much
work. He was unusually gifted and very ambitious, without knowing that he was. For reasons we shall leave
aside he had repressed his ambitious strivings and
hence appeared modest. When he entered the laboratory
of a great chemical firm another member of the staff,
G., a little older in years and higher in rank than C.,
took him under his wing and showed every sign of
friendliness. Because of a series of personal factors—
dependence on others' affection, previous intimidation
concerning critical observation, not recognizing his own
ambition and hence not seeing it in others—C. was
happy to accept the friendliness and failed to observe
that in reality G. cared for nothing but his own career.
And it struck him but dimly that on one occasion G. reported as his own an idea which was relevant for a possible invention but which was really C.'s idea, one that
he had formerly expressed to G. in a friendly conversation. For the flicker of a moment C. was distrustful, but
because his own ambition factually stirred up an enormous hostility in him, he immediately repressed not
only this hostility but with it also the warranted criticism and distrust. Hence he remained convinced that G.
was his best friend. Consequently when G. discouraged
him about continuing a certain line of work he took the
advice at face value. When G. produced an invention
that C. might have made, C. merely felt that G.'s gifts
and intelligence were far superior to his own. He felt
happy to have such an admirable friend. Thus by having repressed his distrust and his anger C. failed to
notice that in crucial questions G. was his enemy rather
than his friend. Because he clung to the illusion that he

was liked, C. relinquished his preparedness to fight for his own interests. He did not even realize that a vital interest of his own was attacked, and consequently could not fight for it, but allowed the other to take advantage of his weakness.

The fears which repression serves to overcome may also be overcome by keeping the hostility under conscious control. But whether one controls or represses hostility is not a matter of choice, because repression is a reflex-like process. It occurs if in a particular situation it is unbearable to be aware that one is hostile. In such a case, of course, there is no possibility of conscious control. The main reasons why awareness of hostility may be unbearable are that one may love or need a person at the same time that one is hostile toward him, that one may not want to see the reasons, such as envy or possessiveness, which have promoted the hostility, or that it may be frightening to recognize within one's self hostility toward anyone. In such circumstances repression is the shortest and quickest way toward an immediate reassurance. By repression the frightening hostility disappears from awareness, or is kept from entering awareness. I should like to repeat this sentence in other words, because for all its simplicity it is one of those psychoanalytic statements which is but rarely understood: if hostility is repressed the person has not the remotest idea that he is hostile.

The quickest way toward a reassurance, however, is not necessarily the safest way in the long run. By the process of repression the hostility—or to indicate its dynamic character we had better use here the term rage —is removed from conscious awareness but is not abolished. Split off from the context of the individual's personality, and hence beyond control, it revolves within him as an affect which is highly explosive and eruptive, and therefore tends to be discharged. The explosiveness of the repressed affect is all the greater because by its very isolation it assumes larger and often fantastic dimensions.

As long as one is aware of animosity its expansion is restricted in three ways. First, consideration of the circumstances as they are in a given situation shows him what he can and what he cannot do toward an enemy or alleged enemy. Second, if the anger concerns one whom he otherwise admires or likes or needs, the anger will sooner or later become integrated into the totality of his feelings. Finally, inasmuch as man has developed a certain sense of what is appropriate to do or not to do, personality being as it is, this too will restrict his hostile impulses.

If the anger is repressed, then access to these restricting possibilities is cut off, with the result that the hostile impulses trespass the restrictions from inside and outside, though only in fantasy. If the chemist I mentioned had followed his impulses he would have wanted to tell others how G. had abused his friendship, or to intimate to his superior that G. had stolen his idea or kept him from pursuing it. Since his anger was repressed it became dissociated and expanded, as would probably have shown in his dreams; it is likely that in his dreams he committed murder in some symbolic form, or became an admired genius, while others went disgracefully to pieces.

By its very dissociation the repressed hostility will in the course of time usually become intensified from outside sources. For instance, if a high employee has developed an anger toward his chief, because the chief has made arrangements without discussing them with him, and if the employee represses his anger, never remonstrating against the procedure, the superior will certainly keep on acting over his head. Thereby new anger is constantly generated.[1]

Another consequence of repressing hostility arises from the fact that a person registers within himself the existence of a highly explosive affect which is beyond control. Before discussing the consequences of this we have to consider a question which it suggests. By definition the result of repressing an affect or an impulse is that the individual is no longer aware of its existence, so that in his conscious mind he does not know that he has any hostile feelings toward another. How then can I say that he "registers" the existence of the repressed affect within himself? The answer lies in the fact that there is no strict alternative between conscious and unconscious, but that there are, as H. S. Sullivan has pointed out in a lecture, several levels of consciousness. Not only is the repressed impulse still effective—one of the basic discoveries of Freud—but also in a deeper level of consciousness the individual knows about its presence. Reduced to the most simple terms possible this means that fundamentally we cannot fool ourselves, that actually we observe ourselves better than we are aware of doing, just as we usually observe others better than we are aware of doing—as shown, for example, in the correctness of the first im-

[1] F. Kuenkel in *Einfuehrung in die Charakterkunde* has drawn attention to the fact that the neurotic attitude calls forth a reaction of the environment, by which the attitude itself is reinforced, with the result that the person is more and more caught, and has greater and greater difficulty in escaping. Kuenkel calls this phenomenon *Teufelskreis*.

pression we get from a person—but we may have stringent reasons for not taking cognizance of our observations. For the sake of saving repetitive explanations I shall use the term "register" when I mean that we know what is going on within us without our being aware of it.

These consequences of repressing hostility may themselves be sufficient to create anxiety, provided always that the hostility and its potential danger to other interests are sufficiently great. States of vague anxiety may be built in this way. More often, however, the process does not come to a standstill at this point, because there is an imperative need to get rid of the dangerous affect which from within menaces one's interest and security. A second reflex-like process sets in: the individual "projects" his hostile impulses to the outside world. The first "pretense," the repression, requires a second one: he "pretends" that the destructive impulses come not from him but from someone or something outside. Logically the person on whom his own hostile impulses will be projected is the person against whom they are directed. The result is that this person now assumes formidable proportions in his mind, partly because such a person becomes endowed with the same quality of ruthlessness that his own repressed impulses have, partly because in any danger the degree of potency depends not only on the factual conditions but also on the attitude taken toward them. The more defenseless one is the greater the danger appears.[2]

2 E. Fromm in *Autoritaet und Familie*, edited by Max Horkheimer of the International Institute for Social Research, has stated clearly that the anxiety with which we react to a danger does not depend mechanically on the realistic greatness of the danger. "An individual who has developed an attitude of helplessness and passivity will react with anxiety to a comparatively small danger."

As a by-function the projection also serves the need for self-justification. It is not the individual himself who wants to cheat, to steal, to exploit, to humiliate, but the others want to do such things to him. A wife who is ignorant of her own impulses to ruin her husband and subjectively convinced that she is most devoted may, because of this mechanism, consider her husband to be a brute wanting to harm her.

The process of projection may or may not be supported by another process working to the same end: a retaliation fear may get hold of the repressed impulse. In this case a person who wants to injure, cheat, deceive others has also a fear that they will do the same to him. How far the retaliation fear is a general characteristic ingrained in human nature, how far it arises from primitive experiences of sin and punishment, how far it presupposes a drive for personal revenge, I leave as an open question. Beyond doubt it plays a great role in the minds of neurotic persons.

These processes brought about by repressed hostility result in the affect of anxiety. In fact, the repression generates exactly the state which is characteristic of anxiety: a feeling of defenselessness toward what is felt an overpowering danger menacing from outside.

Though the steps by which anxiety develops are simple in principle, in practice it is usually difficult to understand the conditions of anxiety. One of the complicating factors is that the repressed hostile impulses are frequently projected not on the person factually concerned but on something else. In one of Freud's case histories, for example, the little Hans did not develop an anxiety concerning his parents but an anxiety concerning white horses.[3] An otherwise very sensible pa-

[3] Sigmund Freud, *Collected Papers*, vol. 3.

tient of mine, after a repression of hostility toward her husband, suddenly developed an anxiety concerning reptiles in the tiled swimming pool. It seems that nothing from germs to thunderstorms is too remote for an anxiety to be attached to it. The reasons for this tendency to detach the anxiety from the person concerned are quite obvious. If the anxiety factually concerns a parent, husband, friend or one in similar close relationship the assumption of hostility is felt to be incompatible with an existing tie of authority, love or appreciation. The maxim in these cases is the denial of hostility all around. By repressing his own hostility the person denies that there is any hostility on his part, and by projecting his repressed hostility to thunderstorms he denies any hostility on the other's part. Many illusions of happy marriage rest on an ostrich policy of this kind.

That a repression of hostility leads with inexorable logic to the generation of anxiety does not mean that anxiety must become manifest every time the process takes place. Anxiety may be removed instantaneously by one of the protective devices we have discussed or shall discuss later. A person in such a situation may protect himself by such means, for example, as developing an enhanced need for sleep or taking to drink.

There are infinite variations in the forms of anxiety which may ensue from the process of repressing hostility. For the sake of a better understanding of the resultant pictures I shall present the different possibilities schematically.

A: The danger is felt to arise from one's own impulses.

B: The danger is felt to arise from outside.

In view of the consequences of repressing hostility

group A appears to be a direct outcome of the repression while group B presupposes a projection. Both A and B can be subdivided into two subgroups.

I: The danger is felt to be directed against the self.

II: The danger is felt to be directed against others.

We would then have four main groups of anxiety:

A. I: The danger is felt to come from one's own impulses and to be directed against the self. In this group the hostility is turned secondarily against the self, a process which we shall discuss later.

Example: phobia of having to jump down from high places.

A. II: The danger is felt to come from one's own impulses and to be directed against others.

Example: phobia of having to injure others with knives.

B. I: The danger is felt to come from outside and to concern the self.

Example: fear of thunderstorms.

B. II: The danger is felt to come from outside and to concern others. In this group the hostility is projected to the outside world and the original object of hostility is retained.

Example: the anxiety of oversolicitous mothers concerning the dangers menacing their children.

Needless to say, the value of such a classification is limited. It may be useful in providing a quick orientation, but it does not suggest all possible contingencies. One should not deduce, for example, that persons developing an anxiety of type A never project their repressed hostility; it can only be deduced that in this specific form of anxiety projection is absent.

With the capacity of hostility to generate anxiety the relation between the two is not exhausted. The process also works the other way around: anxiety in its turn, when based on a feeling of being menaced, easily provokes a reactive hostility in defense. In this regard it does not differ in any way from fear, which may equally provoke aggression. The reactive hostility too, if repressed, may create anxiety, and thus a cycle is created. This effect of reciprocity between hostility and anxiety, one always generating and reinforcing the other, enables us to understand why we find in neuroses such an enormous amount of relentless hostility.[4] This reciprocal influence is also the basic reason why severe neuroses so often become worse without any apparent difficult conditions from the outside. It does not matter whether anxiety or hostility has been the primary factor; the point that is highly important for the dynamics of a neurosis is that anxiety and hostility are inextricably interwoven.

In general, the concept of anxiety I have propounded is developed by methods which are essentially psychoanalytic. It operates with the dynamics of unconscious forces, the processes of repression, projection and the like. If we go into more detail, however, it differs in several respects from the position taken by Freud.

Freud has successively propounded two views concerning anxiety. The first of them was, in short, that anxiety results from a repression of impulses. This referred exclusively to the impulse of sexuality and was

---

[4] When the intensification of hostility through anxiety is realized it seems unnecessary to look for a special biological source for destructive drives, as Freud has done in his theory of the death instinct.

a purely physiological interpretation, because it was based on the belief that if sexual energy is prevented from discharge it will produce physical tension in the body which is transformed into anxiety. According to his second view, anxiety—or what he calls neurotic anxiety—results from fear of those impulses of which the discovery or pursuit would incur an external danger.[5] This second interpretation, which is psychological, refers not to the sexual impulse alone but also to that of aggression. In this interpretation of anxiety Freud is not at all concerned about the repression or non-repression of impulses, but only about the fear of those impulses the pursuit of which would involve an external danger.

My concept is based on a belief that Freud's two views must be integrated in order to understand the whole picture. Thus I have freed the first concept of its purely physiological foundation and have combined it with the second concept. Anxiety in general results not so much from a fear of our impulses as from a fear of our repressed impulses. It seems to me that the reason why Freud could not make good use of his first concept —though it was based on an ingenious psychological observation—lies in his having given it a physiological interpretation instead of raising the psychological question of what happens psychically within a person if he represses an impulse.

A second point of disagreement with Freud is of less theoretical but of all the more practical importance. I fully concur with his opinion that anxiety may result from every impulse of which the expression would in-

[5] Freud, *New Introductory Lectures*, chapter on "Anxiety and Instinctual Life," p. 120.

cur an external danger. Sexual impulses may certainly
be of this kind, but only so long as a strict individual
and social taboo resting on them renders them dangerous.[6] From this point of view the frequency with
which anxiety is generated by sexual impulses is largely
dependent on the existing cultural attitude toward sexuality. I do not see that sexuality as such is a specific
source of anxiety. I do believe, however, that there is
such a specific source in hostility, or more accurately in
repressed hostile impulses. To put the concept I have
represented in this chapter into simple, practical terms:
whenever I find anxiety or indications of it, the questions that come to my mind are, what sensitive spot has
been hurt and has consequently provoked hostility, and
what accounts for the necessity of repression? My experience is that a search in these directions often leads
to a satisfactory understanding of anxiety.

A third point in which I find myself at variance with
Freud is his assumption that anxiety is generated only
in childhood, starting with the alleged anxiety at birth
and proceeding to castration fear, and that anxiety occurring later in life is based on reactions which have
remained infantile. "There is no doubt that persons
whom we call neurotic remain infantile in their attitude
towards danger, and have not grown out of antiquated
conditions for anxiety." [7]

Let us consider separately the elements contained in
this interpretation. Freud asserts that during childhood we are particularly prone to react with anxiety.
This is an undisputed fact, and one for which there are

6 Perhaps in a society such as that described by Samuel Butler in *Ere-
whon*, in which any kind of physical illness is severely punished, an impulse to fall ill would illicit anxiety.

7 Freud, *New Introductory Lectures*, chapter on "Anxiety and Instinctual Life," p. 123.

good and understandable reasons, lying in the child's comparative helplessness against adverse influences. In fact in character neuroses it is invariably found that the formation of anxiety started in early childhood, or at least that the foundation of what I have called basic anxiety was laid in that time. Besides this, however, Freud believes that the anxiety in adult neuroses is still tied up with the conditions which originally provoked it. This means, for instance, that an adult man would be just as much harassed by fear of castration, though in modified forms, as he had been as a boy. No doubt there are rare cases in which an infantile anxiety reaction may with appropriate provocations re-emerge in later life in unchanged form.[8] But as a rule what we find is, in a phrase, not repetition but development. In cases in which the analysis allows us a pretty complete understanding of how a neurosis has developed we may find an uninterrupted chain of reactions from early anxiety to adult peculiarities. Therefore the later anxiety will contain, among others, elements conditioned by the specific conflicts existing in childhood. But the anxiety as a whole is not an infantile reaction. To consider it as such would be to confuse two different things, to mistake for an infantile attitude an attitude merely generated in childhood. With at least as much justification as calling anxiety an infantile reaction one might call it a precocious grown-up attitude in a child.

[8] J. H. Schultz, in *Neurose, Lebensnot, Aerztliche Pflicht*, records a case of this kind. An employee frequently changed positions because certain employers provoked wrath and anxiety within him. The psychoanalysis showed that only those superiors having a certain kind of beard infuriated him. The patient's reaction proved to be an exact repetition of a reaction he had toward his father at three years of age, when the latter attacked his mother in a menacing way.

· CHAPTER 5 ·

The Basic Structure of Neuroses

AN ANXIETY may be fully accounted for by the actual conflict situation. If, however, we find an anxiety-creating situation in a character neurosis we always have to reckon with previously existing anxieties in order to explain why in that particular instance hostility arose and was repressed. We shall find then that this previous anxiety was in turn the result of a pre-existing hostility, and so on. In order to understand how the whole development started we have to go back to childhood.[1]

This will be one of the few occasions on which I deal with the question of childhood experiences. The reason why I shall make less reference to childhood than is customary in psychoanalytical literature is not that I think the experiences of childhood are less significant than do other psychoanalytical writers, but that in this book I am dealing with the actual structure of the neurotic personality rather than with the individual experiences leading up to it.

In examining the childhood histories of great numbers of neurotic persons I have found that the common denominator in all of them is an environment showing the following characteristics in various combinations.

The basic evil is invariably a lack of genuine warmth and affection. A child can stand a great deal of what is

[1] I do not touch here upon the question of how far the tracing back to childhood is necessary for therapy.

often regarded as traumatic—such as sudden weaning, occasional beating, sex experiences—as long as inwardly he feels wanted and loved. Needless to say, a child feels keenly whether love is genuine, and cannot be fooled by any faked demonstrations. The main reason why a child does not receive enough warmth and affection lies in the parents' incapacity to give it on account of their own neuroses. More frequently than not, in my experience, the essential lack of warmth is camouflaged, and the parents claim to have in mind the child's best interest. Educational theories, oversolicitude or the self-sacrificing attitude of an "ideal" mother are the basic factors contributing to an atmosphere that more than anything else lays the cornerstone for future feelings of immense insecurity.

Furthermore, we find various actions or attitudes on the part of the parents which cannot but arouse hostility, such as preference for other children, unjust reproaches, unpredictable changes between overindulgence and scornful rejection, unfulfilled promises, and not least important, an attitude toward the child's needs which goes through all gradations from temporary inconsideration to a consistent interfering with the most legitimate wishes of the child, such as disturbing friendships, ridiculing independent thinking, spoiling its interest in its own pursuits, whether artistic, athletic or mechanical—altogether an attitude of the parents which if not in intention nevertheless in effect means breaking the child's will.

In psychoanalytic literature concerning the factors that arouse a child's hostility the main emphasis is placed on frustration of the child's wishes, particularly those in the sexual sphere, and on jealousy. It is possi-

ble that infantile hostility arises in part because of the
forbidding cultural attitude toward pleasure in general
and infantile sexuality in particular, whether the latter
concerns sexual curiosity, masturbation or sexual games
with other children. But frustration is certainly not the
only source of a rebellious hostility. Observation shows
beyond any doubt that children, as well as adults, can
accept a great many deprivations if they feel the deprivations to be just, fair, necessary or purposeful. A
child does not mind education for cleanliness, for example, if the parents do not put an undue stress on it
and do not coerce the child with subtle or gross cruelty.
Nor does a child mind an occasional punishment, provided it feels certain in general of being loved and provided it feels the punishment to be fair and not done
with the intention of hurting it or humiliating it. The
question of whether frustration as such incites to hostility is difficult to judge, because in surroundings
which impose many deprivations on a child plenty of
other provocative factors are usually present. What
matters is the spirit in which frustrations are imposed
rather than the frustrations themselves.

The reason I stress this point is that the emphasis often placed on the danger of frustration as such has led
many parents to carry the idea still farther than did
Freud himself and to shrink from any interference with
the child lest he might be harmed by it.

Jealousy can certainly be a source of formidable
hatred in children as well as in adults. There is no
doubt about the role that jealousy between siblings [2]
and jealousy of one or the other parent may play in neu-

---

[2] David Levy, "Hostility Patterns in Sibling Rivalry Experiments" in
American Journal of Orthopsychiatry, vol. 6 (1936).

rotic children, or about the lasting influence this attitude may have for later life. The question does arise, however, as to the conditions which generate this jealousy. Are jealous reactions as they are observed in sibling rivalry and in the Oedipus complex bound to arise in every child, or are they provoked by definite conditions?

Freud's observations concerning the Oedipus complex were made on neurotic persons. In them he found that high-pitched jealousy reactions concerning one of the parents were sufficiently destructive in kind to arouse fear and likely to exert lasting disturbing influences on character formation and personal relations. Observing this phenomenon frequently in neurotic persons of our time, he assumed it to be universal. Not only did he assume the Oedipus complex to be the very kernel of neuroses, but also he tried to understand complex phenomena in other cultures on this basis.[3] It is this generalization that is doubtful. Some jealousy reactions do arise easily in our culture in the relations between siblings as well as in those between parents and children, as they occur in every group living closely together. But there is no evidence that destructive and lasting jealousy reactions—and it is these we think of when talking of the Oedipus complex or of sibling rivalry—are in our culture, not to speak of other cultures, so common as Freud assumes. They are in general human reactions but are artificially generated through the atmosphere in which a child grows up.

Which factors in detail are responsible for generating jealousy we shall understand later when discussing the general implications of neurotic jealousy. Suffice it

[3] Freud, *Totem and Taboo.*

to mention here the lack of warmth and the spirit of competitiveness which contribute to this result. Besides, neurotic parents who create the kind of atmosphere we have discussed are usually discontented with their lives, have no satisfactory emotional or sexual relations and hence are inclined to make children the objects of their love. They loose their need for affection on the children. Their expression of affection has not always a sexual coloring, but at any rate it is highly charged emotionally. I doubt very much that the sexual undercurrents in the child's relations to the parents would ever be strong enough to effect a potential disturbance. At any rate, I know of no case in which it was not neurotic parents who by terror and tenderness forced the child into these passionate attachments, with all the implications of possessiveness and jealousy described by Freud.[4]

We are accustomed to believe that a hostile opposition to the family or to some member of it is unfortunate for the development of a child. It is unfortunate, of course, if the child has to fight against the actions of neurotic parents. If there are good reasons for opposition, however, the danger for the child's character formation lies not so much in feeling or expressing a protest, but in repressing it. There are several dangers arising from the repression of criticism, protest or accusations, and one is that the child is likely to take all

---

[4] These remarks presented from a general point of view in disagreement with Freud's conception of the Oedipus complex presuppose that it is not a biologically given phenomenon, but is culturally conditioned. Since this point of view has been discussed by several authors—Malinowski, Boehm, Fromm, Reich—I confine myself to a mere mention of the factors which may generate the Oedipus complex in our culture: lack of harmony in marriage, as a result of conflicting relations between the sexes; unlimited authoritative power of the parents; taboos on every sexual outlet for a child; tendencies to keep a child infantile and emotionally dependent on the parents and otherwise isolating it.

the blame on itself and feel unworthy of love; the implications of this situation we shall discuss later. The danger that concerns us here is that repressed hostility may create anxiety and start the development we have discussed.

There are several reasons, effective in various degrees and combinations, why a child who grows up in such an atmosphere will repress hostility: helplessness, fear, love or feelings of guilt.

The helplessness of a child is often considered merely as a biological fact. Though the child is for long years factually dependent on its environment for the fulfilment of its needs—having less physical strength and less experience than the grown-ups—there is nevertheless too much emphasis on the biological aspect of the question. After the first two or three years of life there is a decided change from the prevailingly biological dependence to a kind of dependence that includes the mental, intellectual and spiritual life of the child. This continues until the child matures into early adulthood and is able to take life into its own hands. There are great individual differences, though, in the degree to which children remain dependent on their parents. It all depends on what the parents try to achieve in the education of their offspring: whether the tendency is to make a child strong, courageous, independent, capable of dealing with all sorts of situations, or whether the main tendency is to shelter the child, to make it obedient, to keep it ignorant of life as it is, or in short to infantilize it up to twenty years of age or longer. In children growing up under adverse conditions helplessness is usually artificially reinforced by intimidation, by babying or by bringing and keeping the child in a stage of emotional dependence. The more helpless a child is made the less will it dare to feel or show opposition, and the longer will such opposition be delayed. In this situation the underlying feeling—or what we may call the motto—is: I have to repress my hostility because I need you.

Fear may be aroused directly by threats, prohibitions and punishments, and by outbreaks of temper or violent scenes witnessed by a child; it may be aroused also by indirect intimidation, such as impressing the child with the great dangers of life—germs, street cars, strangers, uneducated children, climbing trees. The more apprehensive a child is made the less will it dare to show or even to feel hostility. Here the motto is: I have to repress my hostility because I am afraid of you.

Love may be another reason for repressing hostility. When genuine affection is absent there is often a great verbal emphasis on how much the parents love the child and how they would sacrifice for him up to the last drop of their blood. A child, particularly if otherwise intimidated, may cling to this substitute for love and fear to be rebellious lest it lose the reward for being docile. In such situations the motto is: I have to repress hostility for fear of losing love.

Thus far we have discussed situations in which a child represses his hostility against the parents because he is afraid that any expression of it would spoil his relations to the parents. He is motivated by plain fear that these powerful giants would desert him, withdraw their reassuring benevolence or turn against him. In addition, in our culture a child is usually made to feel guilty for any feelings or expressions of hostility or opposition; that is, he is made to feel unworthy or contemptible in his own eyes if he either expresses or feels resentment against the parents or if he breaks rules set up by them. These two reasons for feelings of guilt are closely interrelated. The more a child is made to feel guilty about trespassing on forbidden territory the less will he dare to feel spiteful or accusatory toward the parents.

In our culture the sexual sphere is the one in which guilt feelings are most frequently stimulated. Whether prohibitions are expressed by audible silence or by open threats and punishment, a child frequently comes to feel not only that sexual curiosity and activities are forbidden but that he is dirty and despicable if he indulges in them. If there are any sexual fantasies and wishes concerning one of the parents, these, too, though they remain unexpressed as a result of the forbidding attitude toward sexuality in general, are likely to make a child feel guilty. In this situation the motto is: I have to repress hostility because I would be a bad child if I felt hostile.

In various combinations any of the factors mentioned may bring a child to repress his hostility and eventually produce anxiety.

But does every infantile anxiety necessarily lead ultimately to a neurosis? Our knowledge is not advanced enough to answer this question adequately. My belief is that infantile anxiety is a necessary factor but not a sufficient cause for the development of a neurosis. It seems that favorable circumstances, such as an early change of surroundings or counteracting influences of any sort, may forestall a definite neurotic development. If, however, as frequently happens, living conditions are not of a kind to diminish the anxiety, then not only may this anxiety persist, but—as we shall see later—it is bound gradually to increase and to set in motion all the processes which constitute a neurosis.

Among the factors that may influence the further development of infantile anxiety there is one that I want to consider especially. It makes a great difference whether the reaction of hostility and anxiety is restricted to the surroundings which forced the child into it, or whether it develops into an attitude of hostility and anxiety toward people in general.

If a child is fortunate enough to have, for example, a loving grandmother, an understanding teacher, some good friends, his experience with them may prevent him from expecting nothing but bad from everybody. But the more difficult are his experiences in the family, the more will a child be inclined to develop not only a reaction of hatred toward the parents and other children but a distrustful or spiteful attitude toward everyone. The more a child is isolated and deterred from making other experiences of his own, the more such a development will be fostered. And finally, the more a child covers up his grudge against his own family, as for instance by conforming with his parents' attitudes, the more he projects his anxiety to the outside world and thus becomes convinced that the "world" in general is dangerous and frightening.

The general anxiety concerning the "world" may also develop or increase gradually. A child who has grown up in the kind of atmosphere described will not dare in his own contacts with others to be as enterprising or pugnacious as they. He will have lost the blissful certainty of being wanted and will take even a harmless teasing as a cruel rejection. He will be wounded and hurt more easily than others and will be less capable of defending himself.

The condition that is fostered or brought about by the factors I have mentioned, or by similar factors, is an insidiously increasing, all-pervading feeling of being lonely and helpless in a hostile world. The acute individual reactions to individual provocations crystallize into a character attitude. This attitude as such does not constitute a neurosis but it is the nutritive soil out of which a definite neurosis may develop at any time. Because of the fundamental role this attitude plays in neuroses I have given it a special designation: the basic anxiety; it is inseparably interwoven with a basic hostility.

In psychoanalysis, working through all the different individual forms of anxiety, one gradually recognizes the fact that the basic anxiety underlies all relationships to people. While the individual anxieties may be stimulated by actual cause, the basic anxiety continues to exist even though there is no particular stimulus in the actual situation. If the whole neurotic picture were compared to a state of political unrest in a nation, the basic anxiety and basic hostility would be similar to the underlying dissatisfactions with and protests against the regime. Surface manifestations may be entirely missing in either case, or they may appear in diversified forms. In the state they may appear as riots, strikes, assemblies, demonstrations; in the psychological sphere, too, the forms of anxiety may manifest themselves in symptoms of all sorts. Regardless of the particular provocation, all manifestations of the anxiety emanate from one common background.

In simple situation neuroses the basic anxiety is lacking. They are constituted by neurotic reactions to actual conflict situations on the part of individuals whose personal relations are undisturbed. The following may serve as an example of these cases as they frequently occur in a psychotherapeutic practice.

A woman of forty-five complained about heart-pounding and anxiety states at night, with profuse perspiration. There were no organic findings, and all the evidence suggested that she was a healthy person. The impression she gave was of a warmhearted and straightforward woman. Twenty years before, for reasons which lay not so much in herself as in the situation, she had married a man twenty-five years older than she. She had been very happy with him, had been satisfied sexually, had three children who had developed exceptionally well. She had been diligent and capable in housekeeping. In the past five or six years her husband had become somewhat cranky and sexually less potent, but she had endured this without any neurotic reaction. The trouble had started seven months before, when a likable, marriageable man of her own age had begun to pay her personal attention. What had happened was that she had developed a resentment against her aging husband but had entirely repressed this feeling for reasons that were very strong in view of her whole mental and social background and the basically good marriage relationship. With a little help in a few interviews she was able to face the conflict situation squarely and thereby rid herself of her anxiety.

Nothing can better indicate the importance of basic anxiety than a comparison of individual reactions in cases of character neurosis with those in cases, like the one just cited, which belong to the group of simple situation neuroses. The latter are found in healthy persons who for understandable reasons are incapable of solving a conflict situation consciously, that is, they are unable to face the existence and the nature of the conflict and hence are incapable of making a clear decision. One of the outstanding differences between the two

types of neuroses is the great facility of therapeutic results in the situation neurosis. In character neuroses
therapeutic treatment has to proceed under great difficulties and consequently extends over a long period of
time, sometimes too long a period for the patient to wait
to be cured; but the situation neurosis is comparatively
easily solved. An understanding discussion of the situation is often not only a symptomatic but also a causal
therapy. In other cases the causal therapy is the re-
moval of the difficulty by changing the environment.[5]

Thus while in situation neuroses we have the impression of an adequate relation between conflict situation
and neurotic reaction, this relation seems to be missing
in character neuroses. Because of the existing basic
anxiety, the slightest provocation may elicit the most
intense reaction, as we shall see later in more detail.

Although the range of manifest forms of anxiety, or
the protection against it, is infinite and varies with each
individual, the basic anxiety is more or less the same
everywhere, varying only in extent and intensity. It
may be roughly described as a feeling of being small,
insignificant, helpless, deserted, endangered, in a world
that is out to abuse, cheat, attack, humiliate, betray,
envy. One patient of mine expressed this feeling in a picture she drew spontaneously, in which she was sitting
in the midst of a scene as a tiny, helpless, naked baby,
surrounded by all sorts of menacing monsters, human
and animal, ready to attack her.

In psychoses one will often find a rather high degree
of awareness of the existence of such an anxiety. In
paranoid patients this anxiety is restricted to one or
several definite persons; in schizophrenic patients there

[5] In these cases psychoanalysis is neither necessary nor advisable.

is often a keen awareness of the potential hostility of the world around them, so much so that they are inclined to take even a kindness shown to them as implying potential hostility.

In neuroses, however, there is rarely an awareness of the existence of the basic anxiety, or of the basic hostility, at least not of the weight and significance it has for the entire life. A patient of mine who saw herself in a dream as a small mouse that had to hide in a hole in order not to be stepped upon—and thereby gave an absolutely true picture of how she acted in life—had not the remotest idea that factually she was frightened of everyone, and told me she did not know what anxiety was. A basic distrust toward everyone may be covered up by a superficial conviction that people in general are quite likable, and it may coexist with perfunctorily good relations with others; an existing deep contempt for everyone may be camouflaged by a readiness to admire.

Although the basic anxiety concerns people it may be entirely divested of its personal character and transformed into a feeling of being endangered by thunderstorms, political events, germs, accidents, canned food, or to a feeling of being doomed by fate. It is not difficult for the trained observer to recognize the basis of these attitudes, but it always requires intense psychoanalytic work before the neurotic person himself recognizes that his anxiety does not really concern germs and the like, but people, and that his irritation against people is not, or is not only, an adequate and justified reaction to some actual provocation, but that he has become basically hostile toward others, distrustful of them.

Before describing the implications of the basic anxiety for neuroses we have to discuss one question which is probably in the minds of many readers. Is not the attitude of basic anxiety and hostility toward people, described as an essential constituent of neuroses, a "normal" attitude which secretly all of us have, though perhaps in a lesser degree? When considering this question one has to distinguish two points of view.

If "normal" is used in the sense of a general human attitude, one could say that the basic anxiety has indeed a normal corollary in what German philosophical and religious language has termed the *Angst der Kreatur.* What the phrase expresses is that factually all of us are helpless toward forces more powerful than ourselves, such as death, illness, old age, catastrophes of nature, political events, accidents. The first time we recognize this is in the helplessness of childhood, but the knowledge remains with us for our entire life. This anxiety of the *Kreatur* has in common with the basic anxiety the element of the helplessness toward greater powers, but it does not connote hostility on the part of those powers.

If "normal" is used, however, in the sense of normal for our culture, one could say this much: in general experience will lead a person in our culture, provided his life is not too sheltered, to become more reserved toward people as he reaches maturity, to be more cautious in trusting them, more familiar with the fact that often people's actions are not straightforward but are determined by cowardice and expediency. If he is an honest person he will include himself; if not he will see all of this more clearly in others. In short he develops an attitude which is definitely akin to the basic anxiety. There are these differences, however: the healthy mature person does not feel helpless toward these human failings and there is in him none of the indiscriminateness that is found in the basic neurotic attitude. He retains the capacity of bestowing a good deal of genuine friendliness and confidence on some people. Perhaps the differences are to be accounted for by the fact that the healthy person made the bulk of his unfortunate experiences at an age when he could integrate them, while the neurotic person made them at an age when he could not master them, and as a consequence of his helplessness reacted to them with anxiety.

The basic anxiety has definite implications for the person's attitude toward himself and others. It means emotional isolation, all the harder to bear as it concurs with a feeling of intrinsic weakness of the self. It means a weakening of the very foundation of self-confidence. It carries the germ for a potential conflict between the desire to rely on others, and the impossibility to do so because of deep distrust of and hostility toward them. It means that because of intrinsic weakness the person feels a desire to put all responsibility upon others, to be protected and taken care of, whereas because of the basic hostility there is much too much distrust to carry out this desire. And invariably the consequence is that he has to put the greatest part of his energies into securing reassurance.

The more unbearable the anxiety the more thorough the protective means have to be. There are in our culture four principal ways in which a person tries to protect himself against the basic anxiety: affection, submissiveness, power, withdrawal.

First, securing affection in any form may serve as a powerful protection against anxiety. The motto is: If you love me you will not hurt me.

Second, submissiveness can be roughly subdivided according to whether or not it concerns definite persons or institutions. There is such a definite focus, for example, in submission to standardized traditional views, to the rites of some religion or to the demands of some powerful person. To obey these rules or comply with these demands will be the determining motive for all behavior. This attitude may take the form of having to be "good," although the connotation of "good" varies with the demands or the rules that are complied with.

When the attitude of compliance is not attached to any institution or person it takes the more generalized form of compliance with the potential wishes of all persons and avoidance of everything that might arouse resentment. In such cases the individual represses all demands of his own, represses criticism of others, is willing to let himself be abused without defending himself and is ready to be indiscriminately helpful to others. Occasionally people are aware of the fact that anxiety underlies their actions, but usually they are not at all aware of this fact and firmly believe they act as they do because of an ideal of unselfishness or self-sacrifice which goes so far as a renunciation of their own wishes. In both the definite and the general forms of submissiveness the motto is: If I give in, I shall not be hurt.

The submissive attitude may also serve the purpose of securing reassurance by affection. If affection is so important to a person that his feeling of security in life depends on it, then he is willing to pay any price for it, and in the main this means complying with the wishes of others. Frequently, however, a person is unable to believe in any affection, and then his complying attitude is directed not toward winning affection but toward

winning protection. There are persons who can feel
secure only by rigid submission. In them the anxiety is
so great and the disbelief in affection so complete that
the possibility of affection does not enter at all.

A third attempt at protection against the basic anxiety is through power—trying to achieve security by
gaining factual power or success, or possession, or admiration, or intellectual superiority. In this attempt at
protection the motto is: If I have power, no one can
hurt me.

The fourth means of protection is withdrawal. The
preceding groups of protective devices have in common
a willingness to contend with the world, to cope with it
in one way or another. Protection can also be found,
however, by withdrawing from the world. This does not
mean going into a desert or into complete seclusion; it
means achieving independence of others as they affect
either one's external or one's internal needs. Independence in regard to external needs may be achieved,
for example, by piling up possessions. This motivation
for possession is entirely different from the motivation
for the sake of power or influence, and the use made of
the possessions is likewise different. Where possessions
are amassed for the sake of independence there is usually too much anxiety to enjoy them, and they are
guarded with an attitude of parsimony because the only
objective is to be safeguarded against all eventualities.
Another means that serves the same purpose of becoming externally independent of others is a restriction of
one's needs to a minimum.

Independence in regard to internal needs may be
found, for example, by an attempt to become emotionally detached from people so that nothing will hurt or
disappoint one. It means choking off one's emotional

needs. One expression of such detachment is the attitude of not taking anything seriously, including one's
self, an attitude often found in intellectual circles. Not
taking one's self seriously is not to be confounded with
not thinking one's self important. In fact these attitudes may be mutually contradictory.

These devices of withdrawal have a similarity with
the devices of submissiveness or compliance, inasmuch
as both involve a renunciation of one's own wishes. But
while in the latter group renunciation is in the service
of being "good" or of complying with the desires of
others in order to feel safe, in the former group the
idea of being "good" plays no role at all, and the object
of renunciation is attaining independence of others.
Here the motto is: If I withdraw, nothing can hurt me.

In order to evaluate the role played in neuroses by
these various attempts at protection against the basic
anxiety it is necessary to realize their potential intensity. They are prompted not by a wish to satisfy a desire
for pleasure or happiness, but by a need for reassurance. This does not mean, however, that they are in any
way less powerful or less imperative than instinctual
drives. Experience shows that the impact of a striving
for ambition, for instance, may be equally as strong as
or even stronger than a sexual impulse.

Any one of these four devices, pursued exclusively or
predominantly, can be effective in bringing the reassurance wanted, if the life situation allows its pursuit
without incurring conflicts—even though such a one-
sided pursuit is usually paid for with an impoverishment of the personality as a whole. For example, a
woman following the path of submissiveness may find
peace and a great deal of secondary satisfaction in a
culture which requires from a woman obedience to fam-

ily or husband and compliance with the traditional forms. If it is a monarch who develops a restless striving for power and possession, the result again may be reassurance and a successful life. As a matter of fact, however, a straightforward pursuit of one goal will often fail to fulfill its purpose because the demands set up are so excessive or so inconsiderate that they involve conflicts with the surroundings. More frequently reassurance from a great underlying anxiety is sought not in one way only, but in several ways which, moreover, are incompatible with one another. Thus the neurotic person may at the same time be driven imperatively toward dominating everyone and wanting to be loved by everyone, toward complying with others and imposing his will on them, toward detachment from people and a craving for their affection. It is these utterly unsoluble conflicts which are most often the dynamic center of neuroses.

The two attempts which most frequently clash are the striving for affection and the striving for power. Therefore in the following chapters I shall discuss these in greater detail.

The structure of neuroses as I have described it is not, in principle, contradictory to Freud's theory that in the main neuroses are the result of a conflict between instinctual drives and social demands, or their representation in the "super ego." But while I agree that the conflict between individual strivings and social pressure is an indispensable condition for every neurosis, I do not believe it is a sufficient condition. The clash between individual desires and social requirements does not necessarily bring about neuroses, but may just as well lead to factual restrictions in life, that is, to the simple suppression or repression of desires or, in most general terms, to factual suffering. A neurosis is brought about only if this conflict generates anxiety and if the attempts to allay anxiety lead in turn to defensive tendencies which, although equally imperative, are nevertheless incompatible with one another.

· CHAPTER 6 ·

The Neurotic Need for Affection

THERE can be no doubt that in our culture these four ways of protecting one's self against anxiety may play a decisive part in the lives of many persons. There are those whose foremost striving is to be loved or approved of, and who go to any length to have this wish gratified; those whose behavior is characterized by a tendency to comply, to give in and take no steps of self-assertion; those whose striving is dominated by the wish for success or power or possession; and those whose tendency is to shut themselves off from people and to be independent of them. The question may be raised, however, whether I am right in declaring that these strivings represent a protection against some basic anxiety. Are they not an expression of drives within the normal range of given human possibilities? The mistake in arguing this way is in putting the question in the alternative form. In reality the two points of view are neither contradictory nor mutually exclusive. The wish for love, the tendency to comply, the striving for influence or success, and the tendency to withdraw are present in all of us in various combinations, without being in the least indicative of a neurosis.

Moreover, one or another of these tendencies may be a predominant attitude in certain cultures, a fact which would suggest again the possibility of their being normal potentialities in mankind. Attitudes of affection, of mothering care and compliance with the wishes of others are predominant in the Arapesh culture, as described by Margaret Mead; striving for prestige in a rather brutal form is a recognized pattern among the Kwakiutl, as Ruth Benedict has pointed out; the tendency to withdraw from the world is a dominant trend in the Buddhist religion.

My concept is intended not to deny the normal character of these drives, but to maintain that all of them may be put to the service of affording reassurance against some anxiety, and furthermore, that by acquiring this protective function they change their qualities, becoming something entirely different. I can explain this difference best by an analogy. We may climb a tree because we wish to test our strength and skill and see the view from the top, or we may climb it because we are pursued by a wild animal. In both cases we climb the tree, but the motives for our climbing are different. In the first case we do it for the sake of pleasure, in the other case we are driven by fear and have to do it out of a need for safety. In the first case we are free to climb or not, in the other we are compelled to climb by a stringent necessity. In the first case we can look for the tree which is best suited to our purpose, in the other case we have no choice but must take the first tree within reach, and it need not necessarily be a tree; it may be a flag pole or a house if only it serve the purpose of protection.

The difference in driving forces also results in a difference in feeling and behavior. If we are impelled by a direct wish for satisfaction of any kind our attitude will have a quality of spontaneity and discrimination. If we are driven by anxiety, however, our feeling and acting will be compulsory and indiscriminate. There are inter-

mediate stages, to be sure. In instinctual drives, like
hunger and sex, which are greatly determined by physiological tensions resulting from privation, the physical tension may be piled up to such an extent that satisfaction is sought with a degree of compulsion and
indiscriminateness which is otherwise characteristic of
drives determined by anxiety.

Furthermore, there is a difference in the satisfaction attained—in general terms the difference between
pleasure and reassurance.[1] The distinction, however, is
less sharp than appears at first sight. The satisfaction
of instinctual drives such as hunger or sex is pleasure,
but if physical tension has been pent up the satisfaction
attained is very similar to that attained in relief from
anxiety. In both cases there is relief from an unbearable tension. As to intensity, pleasure and reassurance
may be equally strong. A sexual satisfaction, though
different in kind, may be equally as strong as the feelings of a person who is suddenly relieved from an intense anxiety; and, generally speaking, the strivings
for reassurance not only may be as strong as instinctual
drives, but may yield an equally strong satisfaction.

The strivings for reassurance, as discussed in the
previous chapter, contain also other secondary sources
of satisfaction. For example, the feeling of being loved
or appreciated, of having success or influence, may be
highly satisfactory, quite apart from the gain in security. Furthermore, as we shall see presently, the various
approaches to reassurance allow quite a discharge of

---

[1] H. S. Sullivan in "A Note on the Implications of Psychiatry, the Study
of Interpersonal Relations, for Investigation in the Social Sciences" in
American Journal of Sociology, vol. 43 (1937) has pointed out that the
strivings for satisfaction and security present a basic principle regulating
life.

pent-up hostility and thus afford another kind of relief from tension.

We have seen that anxiety can be the driving force behind certain drives, and have surveyed the most important drives generated in this way. I shall proceed now to a discussion in greater detail of those two drives which factually play the greatest role in neuroses: the craving for affection and the craving for power and control.

The craving for affection is so frequent in neuroses, and so easily recognizable by the trained observer, that it may be considered one of the surest indicators for an existing anxiety and its approximate intensity. In fact if one feels fundamentally helpless toward a world which is invariably menacing and hostile, then the search for affection would appear to be the most logical and direct way of reaching out for any kind of benevolence, help or appreciation.

If the psychic conditions of the neurotic person were what they frequently appear to himself to be, it ought to be easy for him to gain affection. If I may verbalize what he often senses only dimly, his impressions are something like this: what he wants is so little, only that people should be kind to him, should give him advice, should appreciate that he is a poor, harmless, lonely soul, anxious to please, anxious not to hurt anyone's feelings. That is all he sees or feels. He does not recognize how much his sensitivities, his latent hostilities, his exacting demands interfere with his own relationships; nor is he able to judge the impression he makes on others or their reaction to him. Consequently he is at a loss to understand why his friendships, marriages, love affairs, professional relations are so often dissatisfactory. He tends to conclude that the others are at fault, that they are inconsiderate, disloyal, abusive, or that for some unfathomable reason he lacks the gift of being popular. Thus he keeps chasing the phantom of love.

If the reader recalls our discussion of how anxiety is generated by a repressed hostility and how it in turn again generates hostility, in other words, how anxiety and hostility are inextricably interwoven, he will be able to recognize the self-deception in the neurotic's thinking and the reasons for his failures. Without knowing it the neurotic person is in the dilemma of being incapable of loving and yet being in great need of love from others. We stumble here over one of those questions that seem so simple and are nevertheless so difficult to answer : what is love, or what do we mean by it in our culture? One may sometimes hear an offhand definition of love as the capacity to give and take affection. Although this contains some truth, it is much too sweeping to be helpful in clarifying the difficulties with which we are concerned. Most of us can be affectionate at times, but it is a quality that may go with a thorough incapacity for love. The important consideration is the attitude from which affection radiates: is it an expression of a basic positive attitude toward others, or is it, for example, born of a fear that one will lose the other, or of a wish to get the other person under one's thumb? In other words, we cannot take any manifest attitudes as criteria.

Although it is very difficult to say what is love, we can say definitely what is not love, or what elements are alien to it. One may be thoroughly fond of a person, and yet at times be angry with him, deny him certain wishes or want to be left alone. But there is a difference be-

tween such circumscribed reactions of wrath or withdrawal and the attitude of a neurotic, who is constantly
on guard against others, feels that any interest they
take in third persons is a neglect of himself, and interprets any demand as an imposition or any criticism as
a humiliation. This is not love. So, too, it is not incompatible with love to offer constructive criticism of certain qualities or attitudes, in order, if possible, to help
correct them; but it is not love to make, as the neurotic
often does, an intolerant demand for perfection, a demand which implies a hostile "woe unto you if you are
not perfect!"

We also consider it incompatible with our idea of love
when we find a person using another only as a means
for some purpose, that is, only or mainly because he fulfills certain needs. This is clearly the situation when the
other person is wanted only for sexual gratification or,
in marriage, only for prestige. But here too the issue is
very easily blurred, especially if the needs concerned
are of a psychic nature. A person may deceive himself
into believing that he loves another even if, for example,
the other is needed only for the blind admiration that
he gives. In such cases, however, the other person is
likely to be dropped suddenly or even may be turned
against, as soon as he begins to be critical, thereby failing in the function of admiration, for which he was
loved.

In discussing the contrasts between what is and what
is not love we must be watchful, however, not to lean
over backward. Though love is incompatible with use of
the loved one for some gratification, this does not mean
that love must be completely and exclusively altruistic
and sacrificing. Nor does that feeling alone deserve the

name of love which does not demand anything for the self. Persons who express any such convictions betray their own unwillingness to give affection rather than a thoroughly worked out conviction. Of course we want something from the person we are fond of—we want gratification, loyalty, help; we may even want a sacrifice, if necessary. And it is in general an indication of mental health to be able to express such wishes or even fight for them. The difference between love and the neurotic need for affection lies in the fact that in love the feeling of affection is primary, whereas in the case of the neurotic the primary feeling is the need for reassurance, and the illusion of loving is only secondary. Of course there are all sorts of intermediate conditions.

If a person needs another's affection for the sake of reassurance against anxiety, the issue will usually be completely blurred in his conscious mind, because in general he does not know that he is full of anxiety and that he therefore reaches out desperately for any kind of affection for the sake of reassurance. All that he feels is that here is a person whom he likes or trusts, or with whom he feels infatuated. But what he feels as spontaneous love may be nothing but a response of gratitude for some kindness shown him or a response of hope or affection aroused by some person or situation. The person who explicitly or implicitly arouses in him expectations of this kind will automatically be invested with importance, and his feeling will manifest itself in the illusion of love. Such expectations may be aroused by the simple fact that he is treated kindly by a person who is powerful and influential, or by one who merely gives the impression of standing more securely on his feet. They may be aroused by erotic or sexual advances, although these may have nothing to do with love. They may feed on existing ties of some sort, which implicitly contain a promise of help or emotional support: family, friends, physician. Many such relations are carried on under the camouflage of love, that is, under a subjective conviction of attachment, when actually the love is only the person's clinging to others to satisfy his own needs. That this is no reliable feeling of genuine affection is revealed in the ready revulsion that appears when any wishes are not fulfilled. One of the factors essential to our idea of love—reliability and steadiness of feeling—is absent in these cases.

A final characteristic of the incapacity for love has already been implied, but I wish to give it special emphasis: disregard of the other's personality, peculiarities, limitations, needs, wishes, development. This disregard is in part a result of the anxiety which prompts the neurotic to cling to the other person. One who is drowning and clings to a swimmer does not usually consider the other's willingness or capacity to carry him along. The disregard is also partly an expression of the basic hostility toward people, the most common contents of which are contempt and envy. It may be covered up by desperate efforts to be considerate, or even sacrificing, but usually these efforts cannot prevent the emerging of certain unwonted reactions. A wife may be subjectively convinced, for example, of her deep devotion to her husband, and yet be resentful, complaining or depressed when the husband devotes his time to his work, his interests or his friends. An over-protective mother may be convinced that she does everything for the sake of her child's happiness, and yet have a fundamental disregard for the child's needs for independent development.

The neurotic person whose protective device is a

drive for affection is hardly ever aware of his incapacity for love. Most such persons will mistake their need
of others for a disposition toward love, whether for individuals or for mankind in general. There is a pressing
reason for maintaining and defending such an illusion.
Giving it up would mean uncovering the dilemma of
feeling at once basically hostile toward people and
nevertheless wanting their affection. One cannot despise a person, distrust him, wish to destroy his happiness or independence, and at the same time crave his
affection, help and support. In order to achieve both
ends, which in reality are incompatible, one has to keep
the hostile disposition strictly removed from awareness. The illusion of love, in other words, while it is the
result of an understandable confusion between genuine
fondness and need, has the definite function of making
the pursuit of affection possible.

There is still another basic difficulty which the neurotic encounters in satisfying his hunger for affection.
Though he may succeed, at least temporarily, in getting
the affection he wants, he is unable really to accept it.
One should expect him to welcome any affection offered
to him, as eagerly as a thirsty person takes to water. In
fact, that does happen, but only temporarily. Every
physician knows the effect of kindness and consideration. All physical and psychic troubles may suddenly
vanish, even though nothing is being done but giving the
patient hospital care and having him thoroughly examined. A situation neurosis, even though it be a severe
one, may disappear altogether when the person feels
himself loved. Elizabeth Barrett Browning is a famous
example of this kind. Even in character neuroses such
attention, whether it is love, interest or medical care,

may be sufficient to release anxiety and thereby improve the condition.

Any kind of affection may give him a superficial reassurance, or even a feeling of happiness, but deep down it either meets with disbelief or stirs up distrust and fear. He does not believe in it, because he is firmly convinced that no one can possibly love him. And this feeling of being unlovable is often a conscious conviction, unshakable by any factual experiences to the contrary. It can, indeed, be taken so much for granted that it never consciously bothers the person, but even when it is inarticulate it is just as unshakable a conviction as if it had always been conscious. Also, it can be concealed by a "don't care" attitude, usually dictated by pride, and then it is likely to create difficulty in digging it out. The conviction of being unlovable is closely akin to the incapacity for love; it is, in fact, a conscious reflection of that incapacity. A person who can be genuinely fond of others will have no doubts that others can be fond of him.

If the anxiety is really deep, any affection offered meets with distrust, and it will immediately be assumed that it is offered from ulterior motives. In psychoanalysis, for example, such patients feel that the analyst wants to help them only for the sake of his own ambition, or that he makes appreciative or encouraging remarks only for therapeutical reasons. One patient of mine considered it a positive humiliation that I offered to see her during the weekend, at a time when she was emotionally upset. Affection shown demonstratively is easily felt as a taunt. If an attractive girl openly shows affection toward a neurotic man he may take it as teasing, or even as a deliberate provocation, since it is beyond his imagination that the girl might be truly fond of him.

Affection offered to such a person not only may meet with distrust but may arouse positive anxiety. It is as if giving in to an affection meant being caught in a spider's web, or as if believing in an affection meant being taken off one's guard while living among cannibals. A neurotic person may have a feeling of terror when he approaches the realization that some genuine fondness is being offered to him.

Finally, evidence of affection may arouse a fear of dependency. Emotional dependency, as we shall see shortly, is a real danger for anyone who cannot live without the affection of others, and anything faintly resembling it may evoke a desperate struggle against it. Such a person must at all cost avoid any kind of positive emotional response of his own, because such a response immediately conjures up the danger of dependency. In order to avoid this he must blindfold himself against the awareness that others are kind or helpful, somehow managing to discard every evidence of affection and insisting, in his own feelings, that the others are unkind, uninterested or even malevolent. The situation created in this way is similar to that of a person who is starving for food yet does not dare to take any for fear that it might be poisoned.

In short, then, for a person who is driven by his basic anxiety and consequently, as a means of protection, reaches out for affection, the chances of getting this so much desired affection are anything but favorable. The very situation that creates the need interferes with its gratification.

· CHAPTER 7 ·

Further Characteristics of the Neurotic Need for Affection

MOST of us wish to be liked, gratefully enjoy the feeling that we are liked, and feel resentment if we are not. For a child the feeling of being wanted is, as we have said, of vital importance for his harmonious development. But what are the particular characteristics of a need for affection that can be considered neurotic?

It is my opinion that in arbitrarily calling this need infantile one not only wrongs children but forgets that the essential factors constituting the neurotic need for affection have nothing whatever to do with infantilism. The infantile and the neurotic needs have in common only one element—their helplessness—though this too has a different basis in the two cases. Apart from this, the neurotic needs grow under quite different preconditions. These are, to repeat: anxiety, feeling unlovable, inability to believe in any affection, and hostility against all others.

The first characteristic, then, that strikes us in the neurotic need for affection is its compulsiveness. Whenever a person is driven by strong anxiety the result is necessarily a loss of spontaneity and flexibility. In simple terms this means that to a neurotic the gaining of affection is not a luxury, nor primarily a source of additional strength or pleasure, but a vital necessity. The difference is one between "I wish to be, and enjoy being,

99

loved," and "I must be loved at any cost"; or the difference between someone who eats because he has a good appetite, can enjoy his food and be discriminating about it, and another person who is near starvation, must take any food indiscriminately, and pay any price for it.

This attitude necessarily leads to an over-evaluation of the factual significance of being liked. It is, in reality, not so terribly important that people in general should like us. It may, in fact, be important only that certain persons like us—those whom we care for, those with whom we have to live or work, or those on whom it is expedient to make a good impression. Apart from such individuals it is fairly irrelevant whether we are liked.[1] Neurotic persons, however, feel and behave as if their existence, happiness and security depended on being liked.

Their desires may be attached to everyone without discrimination, from the hairdresser or the stranger they meet at a party to their colleagues and friends, or to all women, or to all men. Thus a greeting, a telephone call or an invitation, if more friendly or less, may change their mood and their entire outlook upon life. I should mention one problem in this connection: the incapacity to be alone, varying from a slight uneasiness and restlessness to a definite terror of solitude. I speak not of persons who are dull anyway, and easily bored by their own company, but of persons who are intelligent and resourceful and who could otherwise enjoy a number of things by themselves. Frequently, for example,

[1] Such a statement may meet with disagreement in America, where a cultural factor enters into the picture in so far as being popular has become one of the competitive aims, and has thereby gained a significance which it does not have in other countries.

one sees individuals who can work only if someone is around, and are uneasy and unhappy if they have to work alone. There may be other factors in this need for company, but the general picture is one of a vague anxiety, a need for affection or, more accurately, a need for some human contact. These persons have the feeling of drifting forlornly in the universe, and any human contact is a relief to them. One can sometimes observe, as in an experiment, how the incapacity to be alone parallels the increase of anxiety. Some patients are capable of being alone as long as they feel sheltered behind the protective walls with which they have surrounded themselves. But as soon as their protective devices are effectively tackled by analysis, and some anxiety is stirred up, they suddenly find themselves unable to stand being alone any longer. This is one of the transitional impairments in a patient's condition which are unavoidable during the process of analysis.

The neurotic need for affection may be focussed on a single person—husband, wife, physician, friend. If this is the case the devotion, interest, friendliness and presence of that person will acquire inordinate importance. This importance has a paradoxical character, however. On the one hand, the neurotic seeks the other's interest and presence, fears to be disliked and feels neglected if the other is not around; and on the other hand, he is not at all happy when he is with his idol. If he ever becomes conscious of this contradiction he is usually perplexed about it. But on the basis of what I have said it is evident that the wish for the presence of the other person is the expression not of genuine fondness, but only of a need for the reassurance supplied by the fact that the other is available. (Of course a genuine fondness and a need for reassuring affection may go together, but they do not necessarily coincide.)

The craving for affection may be restricted to certain groups of persons, perhaps to one with which there are interests in common, such as a political or religious group; or it may be restricted to one of the sexes. If the need for reassurance is restricted to the opposite sex the condition may superficially appear to be "normal," and will usually be defended as "normal" by the person concerned. There are women, for example, who feel miserable and anxious if they have no man around them; they will start an affair, break it off after a short time, again feel miserable and anxious, start another affair, and so on. That this is no genuine longing for relationship with men is shown by the fact that the relationships are conflicting and unsatisfactory. Rather, these women choose indiscriminately any man; they want only to have one near them, and are not fond of any of them. And as a rule they do not even find physical satisfaction. In reality, of course, the entire picture is more complicated; I am highlighting only that part which is played in it by anxiety and the need for affection.[2]

One may find a similar pattern in men; they will have a compulsion to be liked by any woman and will feel uneasy in the company of other men.

If the need for affection is concentrated on the same sex, this may be one of the determining factors in latent or manifest homosexuality. The need for affection may be directed toward the same sex if the way to the other sex is barred by too much anxiety. Needless to say, this

[2] Karen Horney, "The Overvaluation of Love, A Study of a Common Present-Day Feminine Type" in *Psychoanalytic Quarterly*, vol. 3 (1934), pp. 605-638.

anxiety need not be manifest, but may be concealed by a feeling of disgust or disinterest concerning the opposite sex.

Since getting affection is of vital importance it follows that the neurotic will pay any price for it, mostly without realizing that he is doing so. The most common ways in which the price is paid are an attitude of compliance and an emotional dependence. The complying attitude may take the form of not daring to disagree with or to criticize the other person, of showing nothing but devotion, admiration and docility. If persons of this type do allow themselves to make critical or derogatory remarks they feel anxiety, even though their remarks may be harmless. The complying attitude can go so far that the neurotic will extinguish not only aggressive impulses but all tendencies toward self-assertion, will let himself be abused and will make any sacrifice, no matter how detrimental this may be. His self-abnegation may appear as, for example, a wish to have diabetes because the person whose affection he desires is interested in research in diabetes, implying that having this illness might perhaps win the other's interest.

Closely akin to the attitude of compliance, and interwoven with it, is the emotional dependence which results from the neurotic's need to cling to someone who holds out the promise of protection. This dependence not only may cause endless suffering but may even be wholly destructive. There are relationships, for example, in which a person becomes helplessly dependent on another, even though he is fully aware that the relationship is untenable. He feels as if the world would go to pieces if he does not get a kind word or a smile, he may have an attack of anxiety at the time he expects a

telephone call, and feel utterly desolate if the other is
prevented from seeing him. But he is unable to break
away.

Usually the structure of an emotional dependence is
more complicated. In relationships in which one person
becomes dependent on the other there is invariably a
great deal of resentment. The dependent person resents
being enslaved; he resents having to comply, but continues to do so out of fear of losing the other. Not knowing that it is his own anxiety which creates the situation,
he will easily assume that his subjugation has been
brought about by the other's imposing on him. Resentment growing on such a basis has to be repressed, because the affection of the other is bitterly needed, and
this repression in turn generates new anxiety, with a
subsequent need for reassurance and hence a reinforced
impulse to cling to the other. Thus in certain neurotic
persons emotional dependence produces a very realistic
and even justified fear that their life is being ruined.
When the fear is very great they may seek to protect
themselves against this dependence by not attaching
themselves to anyone.

Sometimes the attitude toward dependence changes
within the same person. After having gone through one
or several painful experiences of this kind he may struggle blindly against everything that bears even a faint
resemblance to dependence. For example, a girl who had
gone through several love affairs, all of which ended
with her being desperately dependent on the particular
man concerned, developed a detached attitude toward
all men, wanting only to have them under her power
without having her feelings involved.

These processes are evident also in a patient's attitude during analysis. It is to his own interest to use

the hour to gain understanding, but he will often ignore his own interest by trying to please the analyst and win his interest or approval. Even though there may be good reasons why he should want to get on quickly—because he suffers or makes sacrifices for the sake of the analysis, or because he has only a limited time for it—these factors at times seem to become totally irrelevant. The patient will spend hours in long-winded tales only to get an approving response from the analyst, or he will try to make each hour interesting for the analyst, be entertaining, show admiration for him. This may go so far that the patient's associations or even his dreams will be determined by his wish to interest the analyst. Or he may become infatuated with the analyst, believing that he cares for nothing but the analyst's love and trying to impress the latter with the genuineness of his feeling. The factor of indiscriminateness is evident here too, unless one assume every analyst to be a paragon of human values, or to be perfectly fitted for the personal expectations of every individual patient. Of course the analyst might possibly be a person whom the patient would love in any case, but even that would not account for the degree of emotional importance which the analyst acquires for the patient.

It is this phenomenon of which people usually think when they speak of "transference." Yet the term is not quite correct, because transference should refer to the sum total of all the patient's irrational reactions toward the analyst, not only the emotional dependence. The problem here is not so much why this dependence takes place in analysis, because persons in need of such protection will cling to any physician, social worker, friend, member of the family, but why it is particularly strong and why it occurs with such frequency. The answer is comparatively simple: analyzing means, among other things, tackling defenses built up against anxiety, and thereby stirring up the anxiety lurking behind the protecting walls. It is this increase of anxiety that causes the patient to cling to the analyst in one way or another.

Here we find again a difference from the child's need for affection: the child needs more affection or help than the adult, because it is more helpless, but there are no compulsive factors involved in its attitude. Only a child who is already apprehensive will cling to its mother's apron strings.

A second characteristic of the neurotic need for affection, also entirely different from the need of the child, is its insatiability. A child, it is true, may nag, demand excessive attention and endless proofs of being loved, but in that case it is a neurotic child. A healthy child, growing up in an atmosphere of warmth and reliability, feels sure that it is wanted, does not require constant proof of that fact, and is contented when it receives the help it needs for the time being.

The insatiability of the neurotic may appear in greediness as a general character trait, shown in eating, buying, window-shopping, impatience. The greediness may be repressed most of the time, and break out suddenly, as for instance when a person who is usually modest about buying clothes, in an anxiety state buys four new coats. It may appear in the more amiable form of sponging, or in the more aggressive form of an octopus-like behavior.

The attitude of greediness, with all its variations and subsequent inhibitions, is called an "oral" attitude [3]

[3] Karl Abraham, "Entwicklungsgeschichte der Libido" in *Neue Arbeiten zur aerztlichen Psychoanalyse*, Heft 2 (1934).

and as such has been well described in analytical literature. While the theoretical preconceptions underlying
this terminology have been valuable, in so far as they
have permitted the integration of hitherto isolated
trends into syndromes, the preconception that all these
trends originate in oral sensations and wishes is dubita-
ble. It is based on the valid observation that greediness
frequently finds its expression in demands for food and
in manners of eating, as well as in dreams, which may
express the same tendencies in a more primitive way,
as for example in cannibalistic dreams. These phenomena do not prove, however, that we have here to do
with originally and essentially oral desires. It seems
therefore a more tenable assumption that as a rule eating is merely the most accessible means of satisfying
the feeling of greediness, whatever its source, just as in
dreams eating is the most concrete and primitive sym-
bol for expressing insatiable desires.

The assumption that the "oral" desires or attitudes
are libidinal in character also needs substantiation.
There is no doubt that an attitude of greediness may
appear in the sexual sphere, in actual sexual insatiability as well as in dreams that identify intercourse with
swallowing or biting. But it appears just as well in ac-
quisitiveness concerning money or clothes, or in the pursuit of ambition and prestige. All that can be said in
favor of the libidinal assumption is that the passionate
intensity of greediness is similar to that of sexual
drives. Unless one assume, however, that every passionate drive is libidinal, it still remains necessary to prove
that greediness as such is a sexual—pregenital—drive.

The problem of greediness is complex and still unsolved. Like compulsiveness it is definitely promoted by
anxiety. The fact that greediness is conditioned by anx-

iety may be fairly evident, as is frequently the case, for example, in excessive masturbation or excessive eating. The connection between the two may also be shown by the fact that greediness may diminish or vanish as soon as the person feels reassured in some way: feeling loved, having a success, doing constructive work. A feeling of being loved, for instance, may suddenly reduce the strength of a compulsive wish to buy. A girl who had been looking forward to each meal with undisguised greediness forgot hunger and mealtime altogether as soon as she started designing dresses, an occupation which she greatly enjoyed. On the other hand, greediness may appear or become reinforced as soon as hostility or anxiety is heightened; a person may feel compelled to go shopping before a dreaded performance, or compelled to eat greedily after feeling rejected.

There are many persons, however, who have anxiety and yet do not develop greediness, a fact which indicates that there are still some special factors involved. Of these factors all that can be said with a fair degree of certainty is that greedy persons distrust their capacity to create anything of their own, and thus have to rely on the outside world for the fulfillment of their needs; but they believe that no one is willing to grant them anything. Those neurotic persons who are insatiable in their need for affection usually show the same greediness in reference to material things, such as sacrifices of time or money, factual advice in concrete situations, factual help in difficulties, presents, information, sexual gratification. In some cases these desires definitely reveal a wish for proofs of affection; in others, however, that explanation is not convincing. In the latter cases one has the impression that the neurotic person merely wants to get something, affection or no affection, and that a craving for affection, if present at all, is only a camouflage for the extortion of certain tangible favors or profits.

These observations suggest the question of whether it is not perhaps the greed for material things in general that is the basic phenomenon, and the need for affection only one way of obtaining this goal. There is no general answer to this question. Craving for possession, as we shall see later, is one of the fundamental defenses against anxiety. But experience shows also that in certain cases the need for affection, though it is the prevailing protective device, may be repressed so deeply that it does not appear on the surface. The greed for material things may then lastingly or temporarily take its place.

In reference to this question of the role of affection three types of neurotic persons can be roughly distinguished. In the first group there is no doubt whatever that the persons crave affection, in whatever form it may appear, and by whatever methods they may obtain it.

Those in the second group reach out for affection but if they fail to get it in some relationship—and as a rule they are bound to fail—they do not reach out immediately for another person, but withdraw from people altogether. Instead of trying to attach themselves to some person they compulsively attach themselves to things, having to eat or to buy or to read or, generally speaking, to get something. Such a change may sometimes take grotesque forms, as in persons who after failing in some love affair start to eat so compulsively that they gain twenty to thirty pounds in a short time; if they have a new love affair they lose this weight again; and if this love affair ends in failure they again

put on weight. Sometimes one can observe the same behavior in patients; after an acute disappointment with
the analyst they start to eat compulsively and gain
weight to such a degree that they are scarcely recognizable, but they lose it again when the relations are
straightened out. Such a greediness about food may also
be repressed, and then it may become manifest in a loss
of appetite or functional stomach upsets of some kind.
In this group personal relationships are more deeply
disturbed than in the first group. They still desire affection, and they still dare to reach out for it, but any
disappointment can break the thread that binds them
to others.

The third group of persons have been stricken so
severely and so early that their conscious attitude has
become a deep disbelief in any affection. Their anxiety
is so deep that they are contented if no positive harm
is done them. They may acquire a cynical, scoffing attitude toward affection and prefer the fulfillment of their
tangible wishes concerning material help, advice, sexuality. Only after much of their anxiety has been released
are they able to desire affection and appreciate it.

The different attitudes of these three groups can be
summarized as: insatiability concerning affection; need
for affection alternating with general greediness; no
manifest need for affection, but general greediness.
Each group shows an increase in both anxiety and hostility.

Coming back to the main trend of our discussion we
have to consider now the question of the special ways
in which insatiability concerning affection manifests itself. The main expressions are jealousy and demands
for unconditional love.

Neurotic jealousy, unlike a normal person's jealousy, which may be an adequate reaction to the danger of losing someone's love, is altogether out of proportion to the danger. It is dictated by a constant fear of losing possession of the person or of his love; consequently any other interest that person may have is a potential danger. This kind of jealousy may appear in every human relation—on the part of parents toward their children who want to make friends or to marry; on the part of children toward their parents; between marriage partners; in any love relationship. The relationship with the analyst is no exception. It is shown there in an intense sensitivity about the analyst seeing another patient, or even about the mere mention of another patient. The motto is, "You must love me exclusively." The patient may say, "I recognize that you treat me kindly; nevertheless, as you probably treat others equally kindly, your kindness to me does not count at all." Any affection which must be shared with other persons or interests is immediately and entirely devaluated.

Disproportionate jealousy is often thought of as conditioned by jealousy experienced in childhood toward siblings or toward one of the parents. Sibling rivalry as it occurs among healthy children, jealousy toward a newborn baby for example, vanishes without leaving any scar as soon as the child feels sure that he does not lose any of the love and attention he has had hitherto. According to my experience, excessive jealousy occurring in childhood and never overcome is due to neurotic conditions in the child similar to those in an adult, as described above. There already existed in the child an insatiable need for affection, rising out of a basic anxiety.

In psychoanalytic literature the relation between infantile and adult jealousy reactions is often expressed ambiguously inasmuch as the adult jealousy is called a "repetition" of the infantile one. If the term means to imply that an adult woman is jealous of her husband *because* she was equally jealous of her mother, it would not seem tenable. The intensified jealousy that we find in a child's relation to parents or siblings is not the ultimate cause of later jealousy, but both spring from the same sources.

Perhaps an expression of the insatiable need for affection still stronger than jealousy is the quest for unconditional love. The form in which this demand most often appears in the conscious mind is, "I want to be loved for what I am and not for what I am doing." So far we might consider this wish nothing out of the ordinary. Certainly, the wish to be loved for ourself alone is not alien to any of us. The neurotic wish for unconditional love, however, is much more comprehensive than the normal one, and in its extreme form it is impossible of fulfillment. It is a demand for love, literally without any condition or any reserve.

This demand includes, first, a wish to be loved regardless of any provocative behavior. The wish is necessary as a security, because the neurotic person secretly registers the fact that he is full of hostility and excessive demands, and hence he has understandable and proportionate fears that the other may withdraw or become angry or vindictive if this hostility should become evident. A patient of this type will express the opinion that it is very easy and means nothing to love someone who is amiable, that love ought to prove its ability to stand any kind of untoward behavior. Any criticism is felt as a withdrawal of love. In the process of analysis resentment may be aroused by an intimation that he may have to change something in his personality, even though that is the purpose of the analysis, because he feels any such intimation as a frustration of his need for affection.

The neurotic demand for unconditional love includes, second, a wish to be loved without any return. This wish is necessary because the neurotic person feels that he is incapable of feeling any warmth or giving any affection and unwilling to do so.

His demand includes, third, a wish to be loved without any advantage for the other. This wish is necessary because any advantage or satisfaction derived from the situation by the other promptly arouses the neurotic's suspicion that the other likes him only for the sake of that advantage or satisfaction. In sexual relationships persons of this type will begrudge the satisfaction which the other person receives from the relation, because they will feel they are loved only for the satisfaction involved. In analysis these patients begrudge the satisfaction which the analyst receives from helping them. They will either disparage the help the analyst has given them or, while intellectually recognizing the help received, will not be able to feel any gratitude. Or they will be inclined to ascribe any improvement to some other source, to a medicine taken or a remark made by a friend. Of course they also begrudge the fees they must pay. While they may recognize intellectually that the fees are a recompense for time, energy and knowledge, emotionally they will consider the paying of a fee as a proof that the analyst is not interested in them. Persons of this kind are likely too to be awkward in making presents, because presents make them uncertain about being loved.

The demand for unconditional love includes, finally, a wish to be loved with sacrifices. Only if the other person sacrifices everything for the neurotic can he really feel sure of being loved. These sacrifices may concern money or time, but may also concern convictions and personal integrity. This demand includes, for example, the expectation that the other should side with him even to a disastrous degree. There are mothers who rather naïvely feel justified in expecting blind devotion and sacrifices of all sorts from their children because they have "borne them in pain." Other mothers have repressed their wish for unconditional love so that they are able to give their children a great deal of positive help and support; but such a mother derives no satisfaction from the relationship to her children because she feels, like the examples already mentioned, that the children love her only because they receive so much from her, and thus secretly begrudges them whatever she gives them.

The quest for unconditional love, in its implications of a ruthless and merciless disregard for all others, shows more clearly than anything else the hostility hidden in the neurotic demands for affection.

In contrast to the normal vampire type, who may be consciously determined to exploit others to the limit, the neurotic person is usually totally unaware of how exacting he is. He has to keep the knowledge of his demands from awareness because of stringent tactical reasons. No one could possibly say frankly, "I want you to sacrifice yourself for my sake without getting anything in return." He is forced to put his demands on some justified basis, such as that he is ill and therefore needs all the sacrifices. Another powerful reason for not recognizing his demands is that it is hard to give them up when they are once established, and realizing that they are irrational is the first step toward giving them up. They are rooted, aside from the bases already mentioned, in the neurotic's profound conviction that he cannot live on his own resources, that all he needs has to be given to him, that all the responsibility for his life rests on others and not on himself. Therefore giving up his demands for unconditional love presupposes a change in his entire attitude toward life.

All the characteristics of the neurotic need for affection have in common the fact that the neurotic's own conflicting tendencies bar the way to the affection he needs. What then are his reactions to a partial fulfillment of his demands, or to a complete rejection?

CHAPTER 8

*Ways of Getting Affection and Sensitivity
to Rejection*

IN CONTEMPLATING how badly such neurotic persons
need affection, but how difficult it is for them to accept
it, one might assume that these persons would thrive
best in an emotional atmosphere of moderate tempera-
ture. But here another complication enters: they are at
the same time painfully sensitive to any rejection or
rebuff, however slight. And a moderate atmosphere, although in one way reassuring, is felt as a rebuff.

It is difficult to describe the degree of their sensitivity to rejection. Change in an appointment, having
to wait, failure to receive an immediate response, disagreement with their opinions, any non-compliance with
their wishes, in short, any failure to fulfill their demands on their own terms, is felt as a rebuff. And a rebuff not only throws them back on their basic anxiety,
but is also considered equivalent to humiliation. I shall
explain later why they feel it as a humiliation. Because a
rebuff does have this content of humiliation it arouses a
tremendous rage, which may emerge into the open; for
example, a girl whose cat was not responsive to her
caresses became furious and threw the cat against the
wall. If they are made to wait they interpret it as being
considered so insignificant that it is not necessary to be
punctual with them; and this may stimulate outbreaks
of hostility or result in a complete withdrawal of all

feelings, so that they are cold and unresponsive, even though, a few minutes before, they may have been looking forward eagerly to the meeting.

More often the connection between feeling rebuffed and feeling irritated remains unconscious. This happens all the more easily since the rebuff may have been so slight as to escape conscious awareness. Then a person will feel irritable, or become spiteful and vindictive or feel fatigued or depressed or have a headache, without the remotest suspicion why. Moreover, the hostile reaction may occur not only to a rejection, or to what is felt to be a rejection, but also to the anticipation of a rejection. A person may, for example, ask a question angrily, because in his mind he has already anticipated a refusal. He may refrain from sending flowers to his girl, because he anticipates her sensing ulterior motives in the gift. He may for the same reason be extremely afraid of expressing any positive feeling, a fondness, a gratitude, an appreciation, and thereby appear to himself and others colder and more hard-boiled than he really is. Or he may scoff at women, thus taking revenge for an anticipated rebuff.

The fear of rejection, if strongly developed, may lead a person to avoid exposing himself to any possibility of denial. This avoidance may extend from not asking for matches when buying cigarettes to not asking for a job. Persons who fear any possible rejection will avoid making advances to a man or woman whom they like, as long as they are not absolutely certain of not meeting with a rejection. Men of this type usually resent having to ask girls for a dance, because they are afraid the girl may accept only for the sake of being polite; and they think women are much better off in this regard, because they need not take the initiative.

In other words, the fear of rebuff may lead to a series of severe inhibitions falling in the category of timidity. The timidity serves as a defense against exposing one's self to rebuff. The conviction of being unlovable is used as the same kind of defense. It is as if persons of this type said to themselves, "People do not like me anyhow, so I had better stay in the corner, and thereby protect myself against any possible rejection." The fear of rebuff is thus a grave handicap to the wish for affection, because it prevents a person from letting others feel or know that he would like to have some attention. Moreover the hostility provoked by a feeling of being rebuffed contributes a great deal toward keeping the anxiety alert or even reinforcing it. It is an important factor in establishing a "vicious circle" which is difficult to escape from.

This vicious circle formed by the various implications of the neurotic need for affection may be roughly schematized as follows: anxiety; excessive need for affection, including demands for exclusive and unconditional love; a feeling of rebuff if these demands are not fulfilled; reaction to the rebuff with intense hostility; need to repress the hostility because of fear of losing the affection; the tension of a diffuse rage; increased anxiety; increased need for reassurance. . . . Thus the very means which serve to reassure against anxiety create in turn new hostility and new anxiety.

The formation of a vicious circle is typical not only in the context in which it has been discussed here; generally speaking it is one of the most important processes in neuroses. Any protective device may have, in addition to its reassuring quality, the quality of creating new anxiety. A person may take to drinking in order to allay his anxiety, and then get the fear that drinking, too, will harm him. Or he may masturbate in order to release his anxiety, and then become afraid that masturbation will make him ill. Or he may undergo some treatment for his anxiety, and soon grow apprehensive lest the treatment harm him. The formation of vicious circles is the main reason why severe neuroses are bound to become worse, even though there is no change in external conditions. Uncovering the vicious circles, with all their implications, is one of the important tasks of psychoanalysis. The neurotic himself cannot grasp them. He notices their results only in the form of a feeling that he is trapped in a hopeless situation. This feeling of being trapped is his response to entanglements which he cannot break through. Any way that seems to lead out drags him again into new dangers.

The question arises as to what ways are open, despite all the internal difficulties, for the neurotic to obtain the affection he is determined to have. There are really two problems to be solved: first, how to obtain the necessary affection; and second, how to justify to himself and to others the demand for it. We may roughly describe the various possible means of getting affection as: bribery; an appeal to pity; an appeal to justice; and finally threats. Such a classification, of course, like all such enumerations of psychological factors, is not rigidly categorical but is only an indication of general trends. These various means are not mutually exclusive. Several of them may be employed simultaneously or in alternation, depending on the situation as well as on the entire character structure, and depending on the degree of hostility. In fact the sequence in which these four means of obtaining affection are cited indicates an increasing degree of hostility.

When a neurotic attempts to obtain affection by bribery his motto could be described as, "I love you dearly; therefore you should love me in return, and give up everything for the sake of my love." The fact that in our culture such tactics are employed more frequently by women than by men is a result of the conditions under which women have lived. For centuries love has not only been women's special domain in life, but in fact has been the only or main gateway through which they could attain what they desired. While men grew up with the conviction that they had to achieve something in life if they wanted to get somewhere, women realized that through love, and through love alone, could they attain happiness, security and prestige. This difference in cultural positions has had a momentous influence on the psychic development of man and woman. It would be inopportune to discuss this influence in the present context, but one of its consequences is that in neuroses women more frequently than men will use love as a strategy. And at the same time the subjective conviction of love serves as a justification for making the demands.

Persons of this type are in a particular danger of falling into a painful dependency in their love relationships. Assume, for example, that a woman with a neurotic need for affection clings to a man of a similar type, who withdraws, however, as soon as she approaches him; the woman reacts to such rejection with intense hostility, which she represses for fear of losing him. If she tries to withdraw herself he will again start to court her favor. She then not only represses her hostility but covers it up with an intensified devotion. She will again be rejected and again react, eventually with enhanced love. Thus she will gradually become convinced that she is possessed by an unconquerable "grand passion."

Another device that may be considered a form of

bribery is the attempt to win affection by understanding a person, helping him in his mental or professional development, straightening out his difficulties, and the like. This is in common use by both men and women.

A second means of obtaining affection is by appealing to pity. The neurotic will bring his suffering and helplessness to the attention of others, the motto here being, "You ought to love me because I suffer and am helpless." At the same time the suffering serves as justification for the right to make excessive demands.

Sometimes such an appeal will be made quite openly. A patient will point out that he is the sickest patient and therefore has the greatest right to the analyst's attention. He may be scornful of other patients who present a surface appearance of better health. And he resents other persons who are more successful than he in using this strategy.

In appealing to pity more or less hostility may be intermingled. The neurotic may make a simple appeal to our good nature, or he may extort favors by radical means, as by involving himself in a disastrous situation which compels our assistance. Everyone who has had anything to do with neurotics in social or medical work knows the importance of this strategy. There is a great difference between the neurotic who explains his predicament in a matter-of-fact way, and the one who tries to arouse pity by a dramatic demonstration of his complaints. We may find the same trends in children of all ages, with the same variations: the child may either want to be consoled for some complaint or may try to extort attention by unconsciously developing a situation terrifying to the parents, such as an inability to eat or to urinate.

The use of the appeal to pity presupposes a conviction of inability to obtain love in any other manner. This conviction may be rationalized as a general disbelief in affection, or it may take the form of a belief that in the particular situation affection cannot be had in any other way.

In the third means of obtaining affection—the appeal to justice—the motto can be described as: "This I have done for you; what will you do for me?" In our culture mothers will often point out that they have done so much for their children that they are entitled to unflagging devotion. In love relations the fact of having yielded to wooing may be used as a basis for claims. Persons of this type are often overready to do things for others, with the secret expectation that they will receive in return everything they wish, and they are seriously disappointed if the others are not equally willing to do something for them. I am referring here not to persons who are consciously calculating, but to those to whom any conscious expectation of a possible reward is entirely foreign. Their compulsive generosity can perhaps more accurately be described as a magic gesture. They do to others what they want others to do to them. It is the inordinately sharp sting of disappointment which indicates that expectations of a return were factually at work. Sometimes they keep a sort of mental bookkeeping account, in which they give themselves inordinate credit for sacrifices that are really useless, such as lying awake all night, but minimize or even ignore what has been done for them, thus so falsifying the situation that they feel entitled to demand special attention. This attitude leads to repercussions on the neurotic himself, for he may become extremely afraid of incurring obligations. Instinctively judging others by himself, he fears that others might exploit him if he accepted any favors from them.

The appeal to justice may also be put on the basis of what the neurotic would be willing to do for others if he had the opportunity. He will point out how loving or self-sacrificing he would be if he were in the other's position, and he feels that his demands are justified by the fact that he asks no more from others than he would do himself. In reality the psychology of such justification is more intricate than the neurotic himself realizes. This picture he has of his own qualities is mainly his unconscious arrogation to himself of the kind of conduct he would demand of others. It is not altogether a deception, however, for he has in truth certain self-sacrificing tendencies, arising from such sources as his lack of self-assertion, his identification with the underdog, his impulse to be as indulgent to others as he would have them be to him.

The hostility that may be present in the appeal to justice appears most clearly when the demands are put on the basis of reparation for an alleged injury. The motto is: "You have made me suffer or have damaged me, and therefore you are obliged to help me, take care of me, or support me." This strategy is analogous to the one employed in traumatic neuroses. I have no personal experience with traumatic neuroses, but I wonder whether persons acquiring a traumatic neurosis do not belong in this category and use the injury as basis for demands which they would be inclined to make in any event.

I shall cite a few examples which show how a neurotic may arouse feelings of guilt or obligation in order that his own demands may seem just. A wife becomes ill in reaction to a disloyalty of her husband. She does not express any reproach, perhaps does not even consciously feel it, but her illness is implicitly a kind of living reproach, intended to arouse guilt feelings in her husband and to make him willing to devote all his attention to her.

Another neurotic of this kind, a woman with obsessive and hysterical symptoms, would sometimes insist on helping her sisters with the housework. After a day or two she would unconsciously resent bitterly the fact that they had accepted her help and would have to lie down, with an increase of symptoms, thus forcing the sisters not only to manage without her but to have the increased work of taking care of her. Again, the impairment of her condition expressed an accusation and led to demanding reparations from others. The same person once fainted when one of her sisters criticized her, thus demonstrating her resentment and extorting sympathetic treatment.

One patient of mine, at a certain period of her analysis, became worse and worse, and developed the fantasy that the analysis would leave her a wreck in addition to robbing her of all her funds, and that therefore in the future I should be obliged to take complete care of her. Reactions of this kind are frequent in every kind of medical treatment, and are often accompanied by open threats to the physician. In minor degrees occurrences like the following are common: the patient's condition shows a marked impairment when the analyst goes on a holiday; implicitly or explicitly he would assert that it is the analyst's fault that he has become worse and that therefore he has a special claim on the analyst's attention. This example may easily be translated into the experiences of everyday life.

As these examples indicate, neurotic persons of this kind may be willing to pay the price of suffering—even intense suffering—because in that way they are able to express accusations and demands without being aware of doing so, and hence are able to retain their feeling of righteousness.

When a person uses threats as a strategy for obtaining affection he may threaten injury either to himself or to the other. He will threaten some kind of desperate act, such as ruining a reputation or doing violence to another or to himself. Threats of suicide, or even attempts at suicide, are a familiar example. One patient of mine obtained two successive husbands by this threat. When the first man gave indications of being about to withdraw, she jumped into a river in a crowded and conspicuous part of the city; when the second seemed reluctant to marry, she opened the gas, at a time when she was sure of being discovered. Her manifest intention was to demonstrate that she could not live without the particular man.

Since a neurotic hopes, by his threats, to obtain acquiescence to his demands, he will not carry them out as long as he has hopes of achieving this end. If he loses this hope he may carry them out under the stress of despair and vindictiveness.

· CHAPTER 9 ·

The Role of Sexuality in the Neurotic Need for Affection

THE NEUROTIC need for affection often takes the form of a sexual infatuation or an insatiable hunger for sexual gratification. In view of this fact we have to raise the question whether the whole phenomenon of the neurotic need for affection is prompted by dissatisfaction in sexual life, whether all this longing for affection, for contact, for appreciation, for support is motivated not so much by a need for reassurance as by dissatisfied libido.

Freud would be inclined to look at it that way. He has seen that many neurotic persons are anxious to attach themselves to others and prone to cling to them; and he has described this attitude as resulting from dissatisfied libido. This concept, however, is based on certain premises. It presupposes that all those manifestations which are not sexual in themselves, such as the wish to get advice, approval or support, are expressions of sexual needs that have been attenuated or "sublimated." Furthermore, it presupposes that tenderness is an inhibited or "sublimated" expression of sexual drives.

Such presuppositions are unsubstantiated. The connections between feelings of affection, expressions of tenderness and sexuality are not so close as we sometimes assume. Anthropologists and historians tell us that individual love is a product of cultural development. Briffault [1] suggests that sexuality has a closer affiliation with cruelty than with tenderness, although his statements are not quite convincing. From observations made in our culture we know, however, that sexuality can exist without affection or tenderness, and that affection or tenderness can exist without sexual feelings. There is no evidence, for instance, that the tenderness between mother and child is of a sexual nature. All that we can observe—and that as a result of Freud's discovery—is that sexual elements may be present. We can observe many connections between tenderness and sexuality: tenderness may be the forerunner of sexual feelings; one may have sexual desires while being aware only of tender feelings; sexual desires may stimulate or pass into tender feelings. While such transitions between tenderness and sexuality definitely indicate a close relation between them, it nevertheless seems better to be more cautious and to assume the existence of two different categories of feeling, which may coincide, pass into each other or substitute for each other.

Moreover, if we accept Freud's assumption that dissatisfied libido is the driving force for seeking affection, it would scarcely be understandable why we find the same craving for affection, with all the complications described—possessiveness, unconditional love, not feeling wanted, etc.—in persons whose sexual life from the physical point of view is entirely satisfactory. As there is no doubt, however, that such cases do exist, the conclusion is inevitable that dissatisfied libido does not account for the phenomenon in these cases, but that the reasons for it lie outside the sexual sphere.[2]

[1] Robert Briffault, *The Mothers*, London and New York, 1927.

[2] Cases like these, with definite disturbances in the emotional sphere coexisting with a capacity for full sexual satisfaction, have always been a puzzle to some analysts, but the fact that they do not fit into the libido theory does not keep them from existing.

Finally, if the neurotic need for affection were nothing but a sexual phenomenon, we should be at a loss to understand the various problems involved, such as possessiveness, unconditional love, feeling of being rejected. It is true that these various problems have been recognized and described in detail: jealousy, for example, is traced back to sibling rivalry or the Oedipus complex; unconditional love is traced back to oral eroticism; possessiveness is explained as anal-eroticism, etc. But it has not been realized that in reality the whole range of attitudes and reactions described in the previous chapters belong together, that they are the constituent parts of one total structure. Without recognizing anxiety as the dynamic force behind the need for affection, we cannot understand the precise conditions under which the need is enhanced or diminished.

By way of Freud's ingenious method of free association it is possible, in the process of analysis, to observe accurately the relation between anxiety and the need for affection, particularly by paying attention to the fluctuations in the patient's need for affection. After a period of co-operative constructive work a patient may suddenly change his behavior and make demands on the analyst's time or crave his friendship or admire him blindly, or become exceedingly jealous, possessive, sensitive to being "only a patient." Simultaneously there is an increase in anxiety, showing either in dreams or in feeling rushed or in physical symptoms such as diarrhea or frequent urge to urinate. The patient does not recognize that there is anxiety or that his enhanced clinging to the analyst is conditioned by his anxiety. If the analyst recognizes the connection and presents it to the patient, both will discover together that before the sudden infatuation problems were touched upon which stirred up anxiety in the patient; he may, for example, have felt an interpretation by the analyst as an unfair accusation or as a humiliation.

The sequence of reactions appears to be like this: a problem comes up, discussion of which provokes an intense hostility against the analyst; the patient starts to hate the analyst, to dream that he is dying; he represses his hostile impulses immediately, becomes frightened and out of a need for reassurance he clings to the analyst; when these reactions have been worked through, hostility, anxiety and with them the increased need for affection recede into the background. An enhanced need for affection so regularly appears as the result of anxiety that one may safely take it as an alarm signal indicating that some anxiety has come close to the surface and calls for reassurance. The process described is not at all limited to the process of analysis. Identically the same reactions occur in personal relationships. In marriage, for example, a husband may compulsively cling to his wife, be jealous and possessive, idealize and admire her, though deep down he hates and fears her.

It is justifiable to speak of an exaggerated devotion superimposed on a hidden hatred as an "overcompensation," if one realize that the term gives only a rough description and says nothing about the dynamics of the process.

If for all the reasons presented we refuse to accept a sexual etiology of the need for affection, then the question arises whether it is only incidentally that the neurotic need for affection is sometimes coupled with, or appears altogether as, a sexual desire, or whether there are certain conditions under which the need for affection is felt and expressed in sexual ways.

To some extent a sexual expression of the need for

affection depends on whether or not the external circumstances favor it. To some extent it depends on differences in culture, in vitality and in sexual temperament. And finally it depends on whether the person's
sexual life is satisfactory, for if it is not, he is more
likely to react in a sexual manner than those who have
a satisfactory sex life.

Though all of these factors are self-evident, and have
a definite influence on the person's reaction, they do not
sufficiently account for basic individual differences. In
a given number of persons showing a neurotic need for
affection these reactions vary from individual to individual. Thus we find some whose contacts with others
assume immediately, almost compulsively, a sexual coloring of greater or lesser intensity, whereas in others
the sexual excitability or sexual activities keep within
the range of normal feeling and behavior.

Belonging to the former group are men and women
who slide from one sexual relation into another. A more
intimate knowledge of their reactions shows that they
feel insecure, unprotected, and are quite erratic when
having no relations or when seeing no immediate
chance of having one. Belonging to the same group, yet
having more inhibitions, are men and women who factually have very few relations, but who create an erotic
atmosphere between themselves and other persons
whether or not they feel particularly attracted by them.
Finally, a third group of persons belongs here who are
still more inhibited sexually, yet who are easily excited
sexually and compulsively see a potential sexual partner in any man or woman. In this last sub-group compulsory masturbation may—not necessarily must—take
the place of sexual relations.

There are great variations in this group as to the degree of physical satisfaction attained. What the group has in common, apart from the compulsory nature of their sexual needs, is a definite lack of discrimination in the choice of partners. They have the same characteristics that we have already discussed in our general consideration of persons with a neurotic need for affection. In addition one is struck by the discrepancy between their readiness to have sexual relations, factual or imaginary, and the profound disturbance in their emotional relations to others, a disturbance which is more thorough than in the average person haunted by a basic anxiety. It is not only that these persons cannot believe in affection, but that they actually become deeply perturbed—or, in the case of men, impotent—if love is offered them. They may be aware of their own defensive attitude, or they may be inclined to blame their partners. In the latter case they are convinced that they never met a girl or man who was lovable.

Sexual relations mean to them not only the release of specific sexual tensions, but also the only way of getting human contact. If a person has developed the conviction that for him obtaining affection is practically out of the question, then physical contact may serve as a substitute for emotional relationships. In that case sexuality is the main, if not the only, bridge leading to contact with others, and therefore acquires an inordinate importance.

In some persons the lack of discrimination shows itself in regard to the sex of a potential partner; they will actively seek relations with both sexes, or will passively yield to sexual demands, regardless of whether they are made from a person of the opposite or the same sex. The first type does not interest us here, because though with them too sexuality is put into the service of establishing human contact, otherwise difficult to obtain, the precipitating motive is not so much a need for affection as a striving to conquer, or more accurately, to subdue others. This striving may be so imperative that sex distinctions become comparatively unimportant. Men and women both have to be subdued, sexually and otherwise. But those in the second group, who are prone to yield to sexual advances from either sex, are driven by an unending need for affection, especially by a fear of losing another person through refusing a sexual request, or through daring to defend themselves against any requests made upon them, whether just or unjust. They do not want to lose the other person, because the contact with him is so bitterly needed.

To explain the phenomenon of indiscriminate relations with both sexes on the basis of a given bisexuality is to my mind a misconstruction. There are in these cases no indications of a genuine leaning toward the same sex. The seemingly homosexual trends disappear as soon as a sound self-assertion has taken the place of anxiety, just as indiscrimination in reference to the opposite sex also disappears.

What has been said of bisexual attitudes can also throw some light on the problem of homosexuality. In fact there are many intermediate stages between the described "bisexual" type and a definitely homosexual type. In the history of the latter there are definite factors which account for the fact that he excludes a person of the opposite sex as a sexual partner. Of course, the problem of homosexuality is much too intricate to allow an understanding from one point of view alone. Suffice it to say here that I have not yet seen a homosexual person in whom the factors mentioned in the "bisexual" group were not also present.

In the last few years it has been pointed out by several psychoanalytical writers that sexual desires may be reinforced because sexual excitement and satisfaction serve as an outlet for anxiety and for pent-up psychic tensions. This mechanistic explanation may be valid. I believe, however, that there are also psychic processes which lead from anxiety to increased sexual needs, and that it is possible to recognize these processes. This belief is founded both on psychoanalytic observation and on a study of the history of such patients in conjunction with their character traits outside the sexual sphere.

Patients of this type may become passionately infatuated with the analyst at the beginning, impetuously demanding some return of love. Or they may maintain a considerate aloofness during analysis, transferring their need for sexual closeness to some person outside who, as evidenced by the fact that he resembles the analyst or by the fact that the two are identified in dreams, is made to serve as a substitute. Or finally, such persons' need to establish a sexual contact with the analyst may appear exclusively in dreams or in sexual excitement during the interview. The patients are often utterly amazed by these unmistakable signs of sexual desire, because they neither feel attracted by the analyst nor are in any way fond of him. In fact, sexual attraction emanating from the analyst plays no perceptible role, nor is the sexual temperament of such patients more impetuous or uncontrollable than that of others, nor is their anxiety greater or less than that of other patients. What characterizes them is a deep disbelief in any kind of genuine affection. They are thoroughly convinced that the analyst is interested in them only for ulterior motives, if at all, that in his secret heart he despises them, and that probably he will do them more harm than good.

Because of neurotic hypersensitivity reactions of spite, anger and suspicion occur in every psychoanalysis, but in these patients of particularly strong sexual needs these reactions form a permanent and rigid attitude. They make it seem that there is an invisible but impenetrable wall between analyst and patient. When confronted with a difficult problem of their own their first impulse is to give up, to break off the psychoanalysis. The picture they present in analysis is an exact replica of what they have been doing all their life. The difference is only that before the analysis they were able to escape the knowledge of how thin and intricate their personal relations actually were, the fact that they easily became involved sexually helped to confuse the situation and to lead them to believe that their readiness to establish sexual contacts meant that they were having good human relationships in general.

The attitudes I have mentioned are so regularly found together that whenever a patient at the start of a psychoanalysis begins revealing sex desires, fantasies or dreams concerning the analyst I am prepared to find particularly deep disturbances in his personal relations. It is in accord with all observations on this score that the sex of the analyst is comparatively irrelevant. Patients who have worked successively with a man and a woman analyst may have identically the same curve of reaction toward both. In these cases it may therefore be a grave mistake to take at their face value homosexual wishes expressed in dreams or otherwise.

Thus in general, just as "all is not gold that glitters," so also "all is not sexuality that looks like it." A great part of what appears as sexuality has in reality very little to do with it, but is an expression of the desire for reassurance. If this is not taken into consideration one is bound to overestimate the role of sexuality.

The individual whose sexual needs are enhanced under the unrecognized stress of anxiety is inclined naïvely to ascribe the intensity of his sexual needs to his innate temperament, or to the fact that he is free from conventional taboos. In doing so he commits the same error as those who overestimate their need for sleep, imagining that their constitutions require ten hours of sleep or more, while actually their enhanced need for sleep may be determined by a variety of pent-up emotions; sleep may serve them as a means of withdrawing from all conflicts. The same applies to compulsive eating or drinking. Eating, drinking, sleep, sexuality, all constitute vital needs; their intensity varies not only with the individual's constitution, but with many other conditions, such as climate, absence or presence of other satisfactions, absence or presence of external stimulations, degree of strenuous work, existing physical conditions. But also all of these needs may be increased by unconscious factors.

The connection between sexuality and the need for affection throws light on the problem of sexual abstinence. How well sexual abstinence can be endured varies with the culture and the individual. In the individual it may depend on several psychic and physical factors. It is easy to understand, however, that an individual who needs sexuality as an outlet for the sake of allaying anxiety will be particularly incapable of enduring any abstinence, even of short duration.

These considerations lead to certain reflections on the role that sexuality plays in our culture. We tend to look with a certain pride and satisfaction on our liberal attitude toward sexuality. Certainly there has been a change for the better since the Victorian age. We have greater freedom in sexual relations and a greater capacity for satisfaction. The latter point is particularly true for women; frigidity is no longer considered a normal condition in women, but is generally recognized as a deficiency. In spite of the change, however, the improvement is not quite so far-reaching as we might think, because a great deal of sexual activity today is more an outlet for psychic tensions than a genuine sexual drive, and is therefore to be regarded more as a sedative than as genuine sexual enjoyment or happiness.

The cultural situation is reflected also in psychoanalytical concepts. It is one of the great achievements of Freud that he contributed so much to giving sexuality its due importance. In detail, however, many phenomena are accepted as sexual which are really the expression of complex neurotic conditions, mainly expressions of the neurotic need for affection. For example, sexual desires concerning the analyst are usually interpreted as repetitions of a sexual fixation on the father or mother, but often they are not genuine sexual wishes at all, but a reaching out for some reassuring contact to allay anxiety. The patient, to be sure, often relates associations or dreams—expressing, for example, a wish to lie at the mother's breast, or to return to the womb—which suggest a father or mother "transference." We must not forget, however, that such an apparent transference may be only the form in which a present wish for affection or shelter is expressed.

Even if the desires concerning the analyst were

understood as a direct repetition of similar desires toward the father or mother, this would be no proof that the infantile tie to the parents was itself a genuine sexual tie. There is plenty of evidence that in adult neuroses all the features of love and jealousy, which Freud has described as features of the Oedipus complex, may have existed in childhood, but this is less frequently the case than Freud assumes. As I have already mentioned, I believe that the Oedipus complex is, instead of a primary process, the outcome of several processes which are different in kind. It may be a rather uncomplicated response of the child, provoked by the parents giving sexually tinged caresses, by the child witnessing sexual scenes, by one of the parents making the child the target of blind devotion. It may, on the other hand, be the outcome of a much more complicated process. As I have already said, in those family situations which provide a fertile soil for the growth of an Oedipus complex, there is usually much fear and hostility aroused in the child, and their repression results in his developing anxiety. It seems probable to me that in these cases the Oedipus complex is brought about by the child clinging to one parent for the sake of reassurance. In fact a fully developed Oedipus complex, as Freud has described it, shows all the trends—such as excessive demands for unconditional love, jealousy, possessiveness, hatred because of rejection—that are characteristic of the neurotic need for affection. The Oedipus complex in these cases is not then the origin of the neurosis, but is itself a neurotic formation.

· CHAPTER 10 ·

The Quest for Power, Prestige and Possession

THE QUEST for affection is one way frequently used in our culture for obtaining reassurance against anxiety. The quest for power, prestige and possession is another.

I should probably explain why I discuss power, prestige and possession as aspects of a single problem. In detail it certainly makes a big difference for a personality whether the prevailing tendency is for one or another of these goals. Which of the goals prevails in the neurotic's striving for reassurance depends on external circumstances as well as on differences in individual gifts and psychic structure. If I deal with them as a unity it is because they all have something in common which distinguishes them from the need for affection. Winning affection means obtaining reassurance through intensified contact with others, while striving for power, prestige and possession means obtaining reassurance through loosening of the contact with others and through fortifying one's own position.

The wish to dominate, to win prestige, to acquire wealth, is certainly not in itself a neurotic trend, just as the wish for affection is not in itself neurotic. In order to understand the characteristics of the neurotic striving in this direction it should be compared with the normal. The feeling of power, for example, may in a normal person be born of the realization of his own superior strength, whether it be physical strength or ability, mental capacities, maturity or wisdom. Or his striving for power may be connected with some particular cause: family, political or professional group, native land, a religious or scientific idea. The neurotic striving for power, however, is born out of anxiety, hatred and feelings of inferiority. To put it categorically, the normal striving for power is born of strength, the neurotic of weakness.

A cultural factor is also involved. Individual power, prestige and possession do not play a role in every culture. With the Pueblo Indians, for instance, striving for prestige is definitely discouraged, and there is but little difference in individual possessions, and thus this striving too has little importance. In that culture it would be meaningless to strive for any kind of dominance as a means of reassurance. That neurotics in our culture choose this way results from the fact that in our social structure power, prestige and possession can give a feeling of greater security.

In searching for the conditions which produce a striving for these ends it becomes apparent that such a striving usually develops only when it has proved impossible to find reassurance for the underlying anxiety through affection. I shall cite an example which shows how such a striving can develop, in the form of ambition, when the need for affection is thwarted.

A girl was strongly attached to her brother who was four years older than she. They had indulged in tenderness of a more or less sexual character, but when the girl was eight years old her brother suddenly rejected her, pointing out that they were now too old for that sort of play. Soon after this experience the girl de-

veloped a sudden fierce ambition at school. It was
caused certainly by a disappointment in her quest for
affection and this was all the more painful as this child
had not many people to cling to. The father was indifferent to his children, and the mother conspicuously
preferred the brother. But it was not only disappointment that she felt, but also a terrible blow to her pride.
She did not realize that the change in the brother's attitude was caused simply by his approaching puberty.
Therefore she felt ashamed and humiliated, and so
much the more since her self-confidence had in any case
stood on too insecure a basis. The mother had not wanted
her in the first place, and she was made to feel insignificant because the mother, a beautiful woman, was much
admired by everyone; besides, the brother was not only
preferred by the mother but also enjoyed her confidence. The marriage of the parents was unhappy and
the mother discussed all her troubles with the brother.
Thus the girl felt completely left out. She made one
more attempt to get the affection she needed: she fell in
love with a boy whom she met on a trip immediately
after the painful experience with her brother, was quite
elated and began spinning glorious fantasies about this
boy. When he dropped out of sight she reacted to the
new disappointment by becoming depressed.

As quite frequently happens in situations of this
kind, the parents and the family physician ascribed her
condition to her being in too high a class at school. They
took her out of school, sent her to a summer resort for
recreation, and then put her in a class a year below the
one she had been in before. It was then, at the age of
nine, that she showed an ambition of a rather desperate
character. She could not endure being any but first in
her class. At the same time her relations with other

girls, which had formerly been friendly, became visibly impaired.

This example illustrates the typical factors that combine to generate a neurotic ambition: from the beginning she felt insecure because she felt unwanted; considerable antagonism was created, which could not be expressed because the mother, the dominant figure in the family, demanded blind admiration; the repressed hatred generated a great deal of anxiety; her self-esteem had never had a chance to grow, she had been humiliated on several occasions, and she felt definitely stigmatized by the experience with her brother; attempts to reach out for affection as a means of reassurance had failed.

The neurotic strivings for power, prestige and possession serve not only as a protection against anxiety, but also as a channel through which repressed hostility can be discharged. I shall discuss first how each of these strivings offers a special protection against anxiety, and then the particular ways in which it can serve to liberate hostility.

The striving for power serves in the first place as a protection against helplessness, which as we have seen is one of the basic elements in anxiety. The neurotic is so averse to any remote appearance of helplessness or weakness in himself that he will shun situations which the normal person considers entirely commonplace, such as any acceptance of guidance, advice, or help, any kind of dependence on persons or circumstances, any giving in to or agreeing with others. This protest against helplessness does not arise in all its intensity at once, but increases gradually; the more the neurotic feels factually handicapped by his inhibitions, the less he is factually able to assert himself. The weaker he factually becomes the more anxiously he has to avoid anything that has a faint resemblance to weakness.

In the second place, the neurotic striving for power serves as a protection against the danger of feeling or being regarded as insignificant. The neurotic develops a rigid and irrational ideal of strength which makes him believe he should be able to master any situation, no matter how difficult, and should master it right away. This ideal becomes linked with pride, and as a consequence the neurotic considers weakness not only as a danger but also as a disgrace. He classifies people as either "strong" or "weak," admiring the former and despising the latter. He goes to extremes also in what he considers to be weakness. He has more or less contempt for all persons who agree with him or give in to his wishes, who have inhibitions or do not control their emotions so closely that they always show an impassive face. He despises the same qualities in himself as well. He feels humiliated if he has to recognize the existence of an anxiety or an inhibition in himself, and thus despises himself for having a neurosis and is anxious to keep this fact a secret. He also despises himself for not being able to cope with it alone.

The particular forms that such a striving for power will take depend upon what lack of power is most feared or despised. I shall mention a few expressions of this striving that are especially frequent.

For one, the neurotic will desire to have control over others as well as over himself. He wants nothing to happen that he has not initiated or approved of. This quest for control may take the attenuated form of consciously permitting the other to have full freedom, but insisting on knowing about everything he does, and feeling irritated if anything is kept a secret. Tendencies to control may be repressed to such a degree that not only the person himself, but even those about him, may be convinced of his great generosity in allowing freedom to the other. If a person represses his desire for control so completely he may, however, become depressed or have severe headaches or stomach upsets every time the other has an appointment with other friends or unexpectedly comes home late. Not knowing the cause of the disturbances he may accredit them to weather conditions, to an error in diet or similar irrelevant conditions. Much of what appears as curiosity is determined by a secret wish to control the situation.

Also persons of this type are inclined to want to be right all the time, and are irritated at being proved wrong, even if only in an insignificant detail. They have to know everything better than anyone else, an attitude which may at times be embarrassingly conspicuous. Persons who are otherwise serious and dependable, when confronted with a question to which they do not know the answer, may pretend to know, or may invent something, even if ignorance in this particular instance would not discredit them. Sometimes the emphasis is on the need to know in advance what will happen, to anticipate and predict every possibility. This attitude may go with a distaste for any situation involving uncontrollable factors. No risk should be taken. The emphasis on self-control shows in an aversion to being carried away by any feelings. The attraction which a neurotic woman feels for a man may suddenly turn into contempt if he falls in love with her. Patients of this type find it hard to allow themselves much drift in free associations, because that would mean losing control and letting themselves be carried into unknown territory.

Another attitude that may characterize the neurotic

in his striving for power is the desire to have his own way. It may be a constant source of acute irritation to him if others do not do exactly what he expects of them and exactly at the time he expects it. The attitude of impatience is closely connected with this aspect of the striving for power. Any kind of delay, any enforced waiting, even if only for traffic lights, will become a source of irritation. More often than not the neurotic himself is not aware of the existence, or at least of the extent, of his bossing attitude. It is a fact definitely to his interest not to recognize it and not to change it, because it has important protective functions. Nor should others recognize it, because if they do there is a danger of losing their affection.

This lack of awareness has important implications for love relationships. If a lover or husband does not exactly live up to expectations, if he is late, does not telephone, goes out of town, a neurotic woman feels that he does not love her. Instead of recognizing that what she feels is a plain anger reaction to a lack of compliance with wishes of her own, which as often as not are inarticulate, she interprets the situation as evidence that she is unwanted. This fallacy is very frequent indeed in our culture, and it contributes greatly to the feeling of being unwanted which is often a crucial factor in neuroses. As a rule it is learned from parents. A dominating mother feeling resentment about a child's disobedience will believe, and declare, that the child does not love her. A queer contradiction often arises on this basis which may considerably frustrate any love relationships. Neurotic girls cannot love a "weak" man because of their contempt for any weakness; but neither can they cope with a "strong" man because they expect their partner always to give in. Hence what they secretly look for is the hero, the superstrong man, who at the same time is so weak that he will bend to all their wishes without hesitance.

Another attitude in the striving for power is that of never giving in. Agreeing with an opinion or accepting advice, even if they are considered right, is felt as a weakness, and the mere idea of doing so provokes rebellion. Persons for whom this attitude is important are inclined to lean over backward and, out of sheer fear of giving in, compulsively take the opposite stand. The most general expression of this attitude is the neurotic's secret insistence that the world should adapt itself to him instead of his adapting himself to the world. One of the basic difficulties in psychoanalytic therapy comes from this source. The ultimate reason for a patient's analysis is not the gaining of knowledge or insight, but the use of this insight in order to change his attitudes. In spite of recognizing that a change would be for his own good, a neurotic of this type abhors this prospect of changing because it implies for him a final giving in. The incapacity to do this has implications also for love relationships. Love, whatever else it may mean, always implies surrender, giving in to the lover as well as to one's own feelings. The more a person, whether man or woman, is incapable of such giving in, the more unsatisfactory will be his love relationships. This same factor may have a bearing also on frigidity, inasmuch as having an orgasm presupposes just this capacity of completely letting go.

The influence which we have seen that the striving for power has on love relations allows us to understand more completely many of the implications of the neurotic need for affection. Many of the attitudes involved in the striving for affection cannot be wholly understood without considering the part that is played in them by the striving for power.

The quest for power is, as we have seen, a protection against helplessness and against insignificance. This latter function it shares with the quest for prestige.

The neurotic that falls in this group develops a stringent need to impress others, to be admired and respected. He will have fantasies of impressing others with beauty or intelligence or with some outstanding accomplishment; he will spend money lavishly and conspicuously; he will have to be able to talk about the latest books and plays, and to know prominent people. He will not be able to have anyone as a friend, husband, wife, employee, who does not admire him. His entire self-esteem rests on being admired, and shrinks to nothing if he does not receive admiration. Because of his excessive sensitivity, and because he is continually sensing humiliations, life is a constant ordeal. Often he is unaware of feeling humiliated, because the knowledge would be too painful; but whether aware of it or not, he reacts to any such feeling with a rage proportionate to the pain felt. Hence his attitude leads to a constant generation of new hostility and new anxiety.

For purposes of mere description such a person could be called narcissistic. If he is considered dynamically, however, the term is misleading because, though he is constantly preoccupied with inflating his ego, he does it not primarily for the sake of self-love, but for the sake of protecting himself against a feeling of insignificance and humiliation, or, in positive terms, for the sake of repairing a crushed self-esteem.

The more distant his relations with others, the more his quest for prestige can be internalized; it appears then as a need to be infallible and wonderful in his own eyes. Every shortcoming, whether recognized as such or only felt dimly, is considered a humiliation.

Protection against helplessness and insignificance or humiliation can be had also, in our culture, by striving for possession, inasmuch as wealth gives both power and prestige. The irrational quest for possession is so widespread in our culture that it is only by making comparisons with other cultures that one recognizes that it is not a general human instinct, either in the form of an acquisitive instinct or in the form of a sublimation of biologically founded drives. Even in our culture compulsive striving for possession vanishes as soon as the anxieties determining it are diminished or removed.

The specific fear against which possession is a protection is that of impoverishment, destitution, dependence on others. The fear of impoverishment may be a whip driving a person to work incessantly and never miss a chance of earning money. The defensive character of this striving shows in his inability to use his money for the sake of greater enjoyment. The quest for possession need not be directed only toward money or material things, but may appear as a possessive attitude toward others and serve as a protection against losing affection. As the phenomenon of possessiveness is well known, particularly from its appearance in marriages, where law supplies a legal basis for such claims, and as its characteristics are much the same as those described when discussing the quest for power, I shall not give special examples here.

The three strivings I have described serve, as I have said, not only as reassurance against anxiety but also as a means of releasing hostility. Depending on which striving is dominant, this hostility takes the form of a tendency to domineer, a tendency to humiliate or a tendency to deprive others.

The domineering characteristic of the neurotic striving for power does not necessarily appear openly as hostility toward others. It may be disguised in socially valuable or humanistic forms, appearing for example as an attitude of giving advice, liking to manage other persons' affairs, taking the initiative or lead. But if there is hostility concealed in such attitudes, the other persons—children, marriage partners, employees—will feel it and react either with submissiveness or with opposition. The neurotic himself is usually unaware of the hostility involved. Even if he becomes infuriated when things do not go his way, he still maintains his belief that he is essentially a gentle soul who is annoyed only because people are so ill advised as to oppose him. What actually takes place, however, is that the neurotic's hostility is pressed into civilized forms and breaks out when he does not succeed in having his own way. The occasions of his irritation may be of a kind which other persons would not feel as opposition, such as a mere difference in opinion or a failure to follow his advice. Yet considerable rage may be generated by such trifles. One might consider the domineering attitude a safety valve through which a certain amount of hostility may be discharged in a non-destructive way. Since it is itself an attenuated expression of hostility it provides a means of checking purely destructive impulses.

The rage arising from opposition may be repressed and, as we have seen, the repressed hostility may then result in new anxiety. This may manifest itself in depression or fatigue. Since the occasions which arouse these reactions are so insignificant that they escape attention, and since the neurotic is not aware of his own reactions, such depressions or anxiety states may seem to have no external stimulation. Only accurate observation can gradually uncover the connection between the stimulating events and the subsequent reactions.

A further peculiarity resulting from the compulsion to domineer is the person's incapacity to have any fifty-fifty relationships. He either has to lead or he feels entirely lost, dependent and helpless. He is so autocratic that everything falling short of complete domination is felt as subjugation. If his anger is repressed the repression may result in his feeling depressed, discouraged and fatigued. What is felt as helplessness may, however, be only a circuitous way of assuring dominance or of expressing hostility for not being able to lead. A woman, to cite an example, was taking a walk with her husband in a foreign city. Up to a certain point she had studied a map in advance, and took the lead. But when they came to places and streets she had not studied on the map, and where she consequently felt insecure, she yielded the guidance of the walk altogether to her husband. And although she had been gay and active until then, she suddenly felt overwhelmed by fatigue, and could hardly put one foot before the other. Most of us know of relationships between marriage partners, siblings, friends, in which the neurotic person acts like a slave driver, using his helplessness as a whip in order to compel the other to serve his will, in order to command unending attention and help. It is characteristic of these situations that the neurotic person never benefits from the efforts made for him, but responds only with renewed complaints and renewed demands, or worse, with accusations that he is neglected and abused.

The same behavior can be observed in the process of

analysis. Patients of this kind may ask desperately for help, yet not only will they fail to follow any suggestion, but they will express resentment at not being helped. If they do receive help by reaching an understanding of some peculiarity they immediately fall back into their previous vexation and, as if nothing had been done, they will manage to erase the insight which was the result of the analyst's hard labor. Then the patient compels the analyst to put in new efforts which again are doomed to failure.

The patient may receive a double satisfaction from such a situation: by presenting himself as helpless he receives a sort of triumph at being able to compel the analyst to slave in his service. At the same time this strategy tends to elicit feelings of helplessness in the analyst, and thus, since his own entanglements prevent him from dominating in a constructive way, he finds a possibility of destructive domination. Needless to say, the satisfaction gained in this way is entirely unconscious, just as the technique used in order to gain it is applied unconsciously. All that the patient himself is aware of is that he is in great need of help, and does not get it. Hence the patient not only feels completely justified in his own eyes in acting as he does, but he also feels that he has a good right to be angry with the analyst. At the same time he cannot help registering the fact that he is playing an insidious game and consequently he is afraid of discovery and retaliation. Therefore in defense he feels it necessary to strengthen his position, and he does this by turning the tables. It is not that he is secretly carrying out some destructive aggression, but that the analyst is neglecting, cheating and abusing him. This position, however, can be assumed and maintained with conviction only if he really feels victimized. Not only has a person in this condition no interest in recognizing that he is not maltreated, but on the contrary he has a strong interest in maintaining his belief. His insistence that he is being victimized often gives rise to the impression that he wants to be maltreated. In reality he wants it as little as any of us wants it, but his belief in being maltreated has acquired too important a function to be given up easily.

There may be so much hostility involved in the domineering attitude that it creates a new anxiety. This may then result in such inhibitions as an inability to give orders, to be decisive, to express a precise opinion, with the result that the neurotic often appears unduly compliant. This in turn leads him to mistake his inhibitions for an innate softness.

In persons in whom the craving for prestige is uppermost, hostility usually takes the form of a desire to humiliate others. This desire is paramount in those persons whose own self-esteem has been wounded by humiliation and who have thus become vindictive. Usually they have gone through a series of humiliating experiences in childhood, experiences that may have had to do either with the social situation in which they grew up— such as belonging to a minority group, or being themselves poor but having wealthy relatives—or with their own individual situation, such as being discriminated against for the sake of other children, being spurned, being treated as a plaything by the parents, being sometimes spoiled and other times shamed and snubbed. Often experiences of this kind are forgotten because of their painful character, but they reappear in awareness if the problems concerning humiliation are clarified. In adult neurotics, however, never the direct but only the indirect results of these childhood situations can be observed, results which have been reinforced by passing through a "vicious circle": a feeling of humiliation; a desire to humiliate others; enhanced sensitivity to humiliation because of a fear of retaliation; enhanced wish to humiliate others.

The tendencies to humiliate are deeply repressed, usually because the neurotic, knowing from his own sensitivity how hurt and vindictive he feels when humiliated, is instinctively afraid of similar reactions in others. Nevertheless some of these tendencies may emerge without his being conscious of it: in an inadvertent disregard of others, such as letting them wait, in inadvertently bringing others into embarrassing situations, in letting others feel dependent. Even if the neurotic is completely unaware of wishing to humiliate others or of having done so, his relations with them will be pervaded by a diffuse anxiety which is revealed in a constant anticipation of rebuke or humiliation for himself. I shall return later to such fears, when discussing the fear of failure. Inhibitions resulting from this sensitivity to humiliation often appear in the form of a need to avoid anything which might possibly seem humiliating to others; such a neurotic, for example, may be incapable of criticizing, of refusing an offer, of dismissing an employee, with the result that he often appears overconsiderate or over-polite.

Finally, a tendency to humiliate may be hidden behind a tendency to admire. Since inflicting humiliation and bestowing admiration are diametrically opposed, the latter offers the best means of eradicating or concealing tendencies toward the former. This is the reason also why both these extremes are frequently to be found in the same person. There are several ways in

which the two attitudes may be distributed, the reasons
for the distribution being dependent on the individual.
They may appear separately in different periods of life,
a period of a general contempt for people succeeding a
period of hero-worship; there may be admiration for
men and contempt for women, or vice versa; or there
may be blind admiration for one or two persons, and
just as blind a contempt for the rest of the world. It is
in the process of analysis that one can observe that
the two attitudes in reality exist together. A patient
may at the same time blindly admire and despise the
analyst, either suppressing one of the two feelings or
vacillating between them.

In the striving for possession hostility usually takes
the form of a tendency to deprive others. The wish to
cheat, steal from, exploit or frustrate others is not in itself neurotic. It may be culturally patterned, or it may
be warranted by the actual situation, or it may normally
be considered a question of expediency. In the neurotic
person, however, these tendencies are highly charged
with emotion. Even if the positive advantages he derives from them are slight or irrelevant he will feel
elated and triumphant if he meets with success; in order to find a bargain, for example, he may spend time
and energy entirely disproportionate to the amount
saved. His satisfaction at success has two sources: a
feeling that he has outwitted others, and a feeling that
he has injured others.

This tendency to deprive others takes many forms.
The neurotic person will feel resentment toward a physician if he is not treated gratuitously, or for less than he
is able to pay. He will feel anger toward his employees
if they are not willing to work overtime without pay.

In relations with friends and children the exploiting tendency is often justified by alleging that they have an obligation toward him. Parents may actually destroy their children's lives by demanding sacrifices on such a basis, and even if the tendency does not appear in such destructive forms, any mother who acts according to the belief that the child exists to give her satisfaction is bound to exploit the child emotionally. A neurotic of this kind may also tend to withhold things from others, withhold money which he ought to pay, information which he could give, sexual satisfaction which he has led another to expect. The presence of robbing tendencies may be indicated by repeated dreams of stealing, or he may have conscious impulses to steal, which he checks; he may actually have been a kleptomaniac at some period.

Persons of this general type are often unaware that they purposely deprive others. The anxiety connected with their wish to do so may result in an inhibition as soon as something is expected of them, so that, for example, they forget to buy an expected birthday present, or they become impotent if a woman is willing to yield to them. This anxiety, however, does not always lead to an actual inhibition, but may become apparent in a lurking fear that they are exploiting or depriving others, as indeed they are, though consciously they would indignantly repudiate such an intention. A neurotic may even have this fear concerning certain of his activities in which these tendencies are actually not present, at the same time remaining unaware that in other activities he does exploit or deprive other people.

These tendencies to deprive others are accompanied by an emotional attitude of begrudging envy. Most of us will feel some envy if others have certain advantages which we should like to have ourselves. With the normal person, however, the emphasis lies on the fact that he wishes to have these advantages himself; with the neurotic the emphasis lies on the fact that he begrudges them to others, even if he does not want them at all. Mothers of this kind often begrudge the gaiety of their children and tell them that "those who sing before breakfast will cry before supper."

The neurotic will try to disguise the crudity of his begrudging attitude by putting it on the basis of a justified envy. The advantage of others, whether it concern a doll, a girl, leisure or a job, appears so glorious and desirable that he feels entirely justified in his envy. This justification is possible only with the help of some inadvertent falsification of facts: an under-estimation of what he has himself, and an illusion that the advantages of others are the really desirable ones. The self-deception may go so far as to make him actually believe that he is in a miserable state because he fails to have the one advantage in which another person surpasses him, completely forgetting that in all other respects he would not like to change with the other. The price he has to pay for this falsification is incapacity to enjoy and appreciate the possibilities for happiness that are available. This incapacity, however, serves to protect him from the much-feared envy of others. He does not deliberately keep himself from satisfaction with what he has, as many normal persons who have good reason to protect themselves against the envy of certain persons, and therefore misrepresent their real situation; he does a thorough job of it, and really deprives himself of any enjoyment. Thus he defeats his own ends: he wants to have everything, but in consequence of his destructive drives and anxieties he emerges at the end with empty hands.

It is obvious that the tendency to deprive or exploit, like all the other hostile tendencies we have discussed, not only arises from impaired personal relations but results in further impairment. Particularly if this tendency is more or less unconscious, as is usually the case, it necessarily renders the person self-conscious or even timid toward others. He may behave and feel free and natural toward persons from whom he does not expect anything, but he will become self-conscious as soon as there is any possibility of getting any advantage from someone. The advantage may concern tangible things, such as information or a recommendation, or it may concern something much less tangible, such as the mere possibility of future favors. This is true in erotic as in all other relationships. A neurotic of this type may be frank and natural with men for whom she does not care, but feel embarrassed and constrained toward a man whom she wants to like her, because, for her, obtaining his affection is identified with getting something out of him.

Persons of this type may have an exceptionally good earning capacity, thus leading their impulses into profitable channels. More often, they will develop inhibitions concerning the earning of money, so that they will hesitate to ask for pay or will do a great deal of work without getting an adequate reward, thus appearing to behave more generously than is really the case. They are likely then to become discontented at their inadequate earnings, often without knowing the reason for the discontentment. If the neurotic's inhibitions become so ramified that they pervade his whole personality the result will be a general incapacity to stand on his own feet, and he will have to be supported by others. He will then lead a parasitic kind of existence, thus satisfying his exploiting tendencies. This parasitic attitude will not necessarily appear in the gross form of "the world owes me a living," but may take the more subtle form of expecting others to do him favors, to take the initiative, to give him ideas for his work, in short, expecting others to take the responsibility for his life. The result is an odd attitude toward life in general: he has no clear conception that this is his own life, and that it is up to him to make something out of it or to spoil it, but he lives as if what happens to him were no concern of his own, as if good and evil came from the outside without his having anything to do about it, as if he had a right to expect the good things from others and to blame them for all bad things. Since in these circumstances usually more bad than good is produced, a growing embitterment against the world is almost inevitable. This parasitic attitude can be found also in the neurotic need for affection, especially when the need for affection takes the form of a craving for material favors.

Another frequent outcome of the neurotic's tendency to deprive or exploit is an anxiety that he will be cheated or exploited by others. He may live in a perpetual fear that someone will take advantage of him, that money or ideas will be stolen from him, and he will react to every person he meets with the fear that this person might want something of him. A seemingly disproportionate amount of anger is discharged if he is really cheated, if, for example, a taxi-driver does not take the shortest route, or if a waiter overcharges him. The psychic value of projecting one's own abusing tendencies on others is obvious. It is far more pleasant to feel a righteous indignation at others than to face a problem of one's own. Moreover, hysterical persons often use accusations as a means of intimidation, or bullying the other into feeling guilty and thus letting himself be abused. Sinclair Lewis has given a brilliant description of this kind of strategy in the character of Mrs. Dodsworth.

The aims and functions of the neurotic striving for power, prestige and possession can be very roughly schematized as follows:

AIMS	REASSURANCE AGAINST	HOSTILITY APPEARS IN THE FORM OF
power	helplessness	tendency to domineer
prestige	humiliation	tendency to humiliate
possession	destitution	tendency to deprive others

It is an achievement of Alfred Adler to have seen and emphasized the importance of these strivings, the role they play in neurotic manifestations and the disguises in which they appear. Adler, however, assumes these strivings to be the foremost trend in human nature, not in themselves requiring any explanation;[1] their intensification in neurotics he traces back to feelings of inferiority and to physical inadequacies.

Freud has also seen many of the implications of these strivings, but he does not regard them as belonging together. The striving for prestige he considers an expression of narcissistic tendencies. He would originally have considered the strivings for power and possession, and the hostility involved in them, as deriva-

[1] The same one-sided evaluation of the wish for power is found in Nietzsche, *Der Wille zur Macht.*

tives of the "anal-sadistic stage." Later, however, he recognized that such hostilities could not be reduced to a sexual basis, and assumed them to be an expression of a "death instinct," thus remaining faithful to his biological orientation. Neither Adler nor Freud has recognized the role that anxiety plays in bringing about such drives, nor has either of them seen the cultural implications in the forms in which they are expressed.

· CHAPTER 11 ·

Neurotic Competitiveness

THE WAYS of obtaining power, prestige and possession differ in different cultures. They may come by right of inheritance or they may come from the individual's possession of certain qualities appreciated by his cultural group, such as courage, cunning, capacity to cure the sick or communicate with supernatural powers, mental instability, and the like. They may be acquired also by extraordinary or successful activities, achieved on the basis of given qualities or through the favor of fortuitous circumstances. In our culture inheritance of position and wealth certainly plays a role. If, however, power, prestige and possession have to be acquired by the individual's own efforts he is compelled to enter into competitive struggle with others. From its economic center competition radiates into all other activities and permeates love, social relations and play. Therefore competition is a problem for everyone in our culture, and it is not at all surprising to find it an unfailing center of neurotic conflicts.

In our culture neurotic competitiveness differs from the normal in three respects. First, the neurotic constantly measures himself against others, even in situations which do not call for it. Although striving to surpass others is essential in all competitive situations, the neurotic measures himself against persons who are in no way potential competitors and who have no goal in

common with him. The question as to who is the more
intelligent, attractive, popular, is indiscriminately applied to everyone. His feeling toward life can be compared to that of a jockey in a race, for whom only one
thing matters—whether he is ahead of the others. This
attitude leads necessarily to a loss or impairment of real
interest in any cause. It is not the content of what he is
doing that matters so much as the question of how much
success, impression, prestige will be gained by it. The
neurotic may be aware of this attitude of measuring
himself against others, or he may do it automatically
without being aware of doing it. He is scarcely ever fully
aware of the role it plays for him.

The second difference from normal competitiveness is
that the neurotic's ambition is not only to accomplish
more than others, or to have greater success than they,
but to be unique and exceptional. While he may think
in the comparative his aim is always in the superlative.
He may be perfectly aware of being driven by relentless
ambition. More frequently, however, he either represses
his ambition entirely or partly covers it. In the latter
case he may believe, for example, that he cares not for
success, but only for the cause he is working for; or he
may believe that he does not want to be in the limelight,
but only wants to pull the strings behind the scene; or
he may admit that he was once ambitious, at some period
in his life—that as a boy he had fantasies of being Christ
or a second Napoleon, or saving the world from war,
that as a girl she wanted to marry the Prince of Wales—
but will declare that since then his ambition has sub-
sided altogether. He may even complain that it has re-
ceded too much, and that it would be desirable to recap-
ture some of his old ambition. If he has repressed his
ambition entirely he is likely to be convinced that ambi-

tion has always been quite alien to him. Only when a few protective layers have been loosened by the analyst will he recall having had fantasies of a grandiose nature, or thoughts that flashed through his mind of being the very best in his field or of being exceptionally clever or handsome, or having caught himself feeling amazed that any woman could fall in love with another man when he was around, and, even retrospectively, resenting it. In most cases, however, ignorant of the powerful role ambition plays in his reactions, he does not ascribe any particular significance to such thoughts.

Such an ambition will sometimes be focussed upon one particular goal: intelligence, or attractiveness, or achievements of some kind, or morals. Sometimes, however, the ambition is not centered on a definite goal, but spreads over all the person's activities. He has to be the best in every field he comes in touch with. He may want to be at the same time a great inventor and an outstanding physician and an unequaled musician. A woman may want to be not only the first in her particular field of work but also a perfect housewife and a best-dressed woman. Adolescents of this type may find it hard to choose or pursue any one career, because choosing one means renouncing another, or at least renouncing part of their favorite interests and activities. For most persons it would be difficult indeed to master architecture, surgery and the violin. Also such adolescents may begin their work with expectations that are excessive and fantastic: to paint like Rembrandt, to write plays like Shakespeare, to be able to make an accurate blood count as soon as starting to work in the laboratory. Since their excessive ambition leads them to expect too much they fall short in their achievements, and are thus easily discouraged and disappointed and are soon induced to give up their endeavors and start something else. Many gifted persons scatter their energies this way during their entire life. They have indeed great potentialities for achieving something in various fields, but by being interested and eventually ambitious in all of them they are incapable of consistent pursuit of any goal; in the end they achieve nothing and let their fine faculties go to waste.

Whether or not there is awareness of the ambition there is always great sensitivity to any frustration of it. Even a success may be felt as a disappointment, because it does not quite measure up to high-flown expectations. For example, a success with a scientific paper or book may nevertheless be a disappointment because it does not set the Thames on fire, but arouses only a limited interest. A person of this type after having passed a difficult examination will discount his success by pointing out that others, too, have passed. This persistent tendency toward disappointment is one of the reasons why persons of this type cannot enjoy success. Other reasons I shall discuss later. Naturally they are also extremely sensitive to any criticism. Many persons have never produced more than their first book or their first picture, because they felt too deeply discouraged by even mild criticism. Many latent neuroses first became manifest at the criticism of a superior or the incurrence of a failure, although the criticism or the failure may in itself have been trivial, or at any rate quite out of proportion to the resulting mental trouble.

The third difference from normal competition is the implicit hostility in the neurotic's ambitions, his attitude that "no one but I shall be beautiful, capable, successful." Hostility is inherent in every intense competition, since the victory of one of the competitors implies the defeat of the other. There is, in fact, so much destructive competition in an individualistic culture that as an isolated feature one hesitates to call it a neurotic characteristic. It is almost a cultural pattern. In the neurotic person, however, the destructive aspect is stronger than the constructive: it is more important for him to see others defeated than to succeed himself. More precisely, the neurotic-ambitious person acts *as if* it were more important for him to defeat others than to succeed. In reality his own success is of the utmost importance to him; but since he has strong inhibitions toward success—as we shall see later—the only way that remains open to him is to be, or at least to feel, superior: to tear down the others, to bring them down to his own level, or rather beneath it.

In the competitive struggles of our culture it is often expedient to try to damage a competitor in order to enhance one's own position or glory or to keep down a potential rival. The neurotic, however, is driven by a blind, indiscriminate and compulsive urge to disparage others. He may do this even though he realizes that the others would do him no actual harm, or even when their defeat is distinctly counter to his own interests. His feeling may be described as an articulate conviction that "only one can succeed," which is only another way of expressing the idea that "no one but I shall succeed." There may be an enormous amount of emotional intensity behind his destructive impulses. For example, a man who was writing a play was thrown into a blind fury when he heard that a friend of his was also working on a play.

This impulse to defeat or frustrate the efforts of others may be seen in many relationships. A child with excessive ambition may become impelled by a wish to defeat all his parents' efforts on his behalf. If the parents press him in matters of deportment and social success he will develop a kind of behavior which is socially scandalous. If they concentrate their efforts on his intellectual development he may develop such strong inhibitions toward learning that he appears to be feebleminded. I recall two young patients brought to me who were suspected of being feebleminded, although later they proved to be very capable and intelligent. The fact that they were motivated by a wish to defeat their parents became apparent in their attempts to act in the same way toward the psychoanalyst. One of them pretended for some time not to understand me, so that I became insecure in my judgment of her intelligence, until I recognized that she had been playing the same game with me that she had used against her parents and teachers. Both youngsters had vigorous ambitions, but at the beginning of the treatment the ambition was completely submerged in destructive impulses.

The same attitude may appear toward lessons or toward any kind of treatment. When taking lessons or undergoing treatments it is to the person's interest to profit from them. For a neurotic person of this type, however, or more accurately speaking, for the competitive part in him, it becomes more important to defeat the efforts or thwart the possible success of the teacher or physician. And if he can achieve this goal by merely demonstrating in his own person that nothing has been achieved, he is willing to pay even the price of remaining ill or ignorant, thereby demonstrating to others that

they are no good. It is needless to add that this process
works unconsciously. In his conscious mind such a person will be convinced that the teacher or the physician is
factually incapable, or is not the right person for him.

Thus a patient of this type will be inordinately afraid
that the analyst will succeed with him. He will go to any
length to defeat the analyst's efforts, even though in doing so he obviously defeats his own ends. Not only will
he mislead the analyst or withhold important information, but he may even stay in the same condition or dramatically become worse, as long as he possibly can. He
will not tell the analyst of any improvements, or if he
does it will be only reluctantly, or in a complaining fashion, or he will credit an improvement or any gain in insight to some outside factor, such as a change in tem-
perature, the fact that he has taken aspirin, something
he has read. He will not follow any lead of the analyst,
thus attempting to prove that the latter is definitely
wrong. Or he will bring up as a finding of his own a suggestion of the analyst which he had originally rejected
with violence. This latter behavior can often be observed
in ordinary daily affairs; it constitutes the dynamics of
unconscious plagiarism, and many battles for priority
have such a psychological basis. Such a person cannot
stand the idea that anyone but he should have a new
thought. He will decidedly disparage any suggestion
that is not his own. He will, for instance, dislike or refuse
a movie or a book if it is recommended by a person with
whom he is competing at the time.

When all these reactions are brought closer to awareness in the process of analysis the neurotic may have
open outbreaks of rage after a good interpretation: impulses to smash something in the office or to shout insult-

ing remarks at the analyst. Or after some problems have been clarified he will point out immediately that there are still many problems unsolved. Even if he has improved considerably and recognizes this fact intellectually, he fights against feeling any gratitude. There are other factors involved in the phenomenon of ingratitude, such as the fear of incurring obligations, but one important element in it is frequently this humiliation which the neurotic feels for having to give someone credit for something.

There is much anxiety connected with the defeating impulses because of the fact that the neurotic person automatically assumes that others will feel just as much hurt and vindictive after a defeat as he does himself. Therefore he is anxious about hurting others and keeps the extent of his defeating tendencies from awareness by believing and insisting that they are factually justified.

If the neurotic has a strongly disparaging attitude he has difficulties in forming any positive opinion, taking any positive stand, or making any constructive decision. A positive opinion on some person or matter may be shattered by the slightest negative remark that anyone makes, because it takes only a trifle to stir up his disparaging impulses.

All these destructive impulses involved in the neurotic striving for power, prestige and possession enter into the competitive struggle. In the general competitive struggle that takes place in our culture even the normal person is likely to show these tendencies, but in the neurotic person such impulses become important in themselves, regardless of any disadvantage or suffering they may bring him. The ability to humiliate or exploit or cheat other people becomes for him a triumph of superiority or, if he fails, a defeat. Much of the rage shown by the neurotic if he is incapable of taking advantage of others is due to such a feeling of defeat.

If an individualistic competitive spirit prevails in any society it is bound to impair the relations between the sexes, unless the spheres of life pertaining to man and woman are strictly separated. Neurotic competitiveness, however, produces even greater havoc than the average, because of its destructive character.

In love relationships the neurotic's tendencies to defeat, subdue and humiliate the partner play an enormous role. Sexual relations become a means of either subduing and degrading the partner or of being subdued and degraded by him, a character which is certainly entirely alien to their nature. Often a situation develops which Freud has described as a split in man's love relations: a man may feel sexually attracted only to women below his standards, having neither desire nor potency for women whom he loves and admires. For such a person sexual intercourse is inseparably coupled with humiliating tendencies, so that he immediately represses sexual desires toward one whom he loves, or can love. This attitude is often traceable to his mother, by whom he felt humiliated and whom he wished to humiliate in return, but out of fear hid this impulse behind an exaggerated devotion—a situation which is often described as a fixation. For his further life he finds this solution of dividing women into two groups; the remaining hostility toward women he loves takes the form of factually frustrating them.

If a man of this kind enters a relationship with a woman of equal or superior standing or personality he often feels secretly ashamed of the woman instead of being proud. He may feel extremely puzzled by this reaction, because in his conscious thinking a woman does not lose value by entering a sexual relation. What he does not know is that his impulses to degrade a woman by sexual intercourse are so strong that emotionally she has become despicable for him. Therefore being ashamed of her is a logical reaction. A woman, too, may be irrationally ashamed of her lover, showing it by not wanting to be seen with him or by being blind toward his good qualities, thus appreciating him less than he actually deserves. Analysis reveals that she has this same unconscious tendency to degrade the partner.[1] Usually she has these tendencies toward women as well, but for individual reasons they are more accentuated in her relations with men. The individual reasons for this may be of various kinds: resentment toward a preferred brother, contempt for a weak father, conviction of not being attractive and hence anticipating rejection from men. Also, she may feel too great a fear of women to allow an expression of humiliating tendencies toward them.

Women, as well as men, may be fully aware of being intent upon subduing and humiliating the other sex. A girl may start a love affair with the frank motivation of getting the man under her thumb. Or she may attract men and drop them as soon as they respond with affection. Usually, however, the desire to humiliate is

[1] Dorian Feigenbaum has recorded a case of this kind in a paper which will be published in the *Psychoanalytic Quarterly* under the title, "Morbid Shame." His interpretation, however, is different from mine, for in the last analysis he traces back the shame to penis envy. Much of what in psychoanalytic literature is regarded as castrative tendencies in women, and is traced back to penis envy, is in my opinion the result of a wish to humiliate men.

not conscious. In such cases it may be revealed in many indirect ways. It may, for example, become evident in a compulsive laughter at the man's advances. Or it may take the form of frigidity, by which she shows the man that he is incapable of giving her satisfaction and thus succeeds in humiliating him, particularly if he has himself a neurotic fear of being humiliated by women. The reverse side of the picture—often to be seen in the same person—is a feeling of being abused, degraded and humiliated by sexual relations. In the Victorian age it was the cultural pattern for a woman o feel sexual relations as a humiliation, a feeling that was attenuated if the relation was legalized and decently frigid. This cultural influence has become weaker in the last thirty years but is still sufficiently strong to account for the fact that women more frequently than men feel that sexual relations hurt their dignity. This too may result in frigidity or in keeping away from men altogether, despite wishes for contact with them. The woman may find secondary satisfaction in this attitude by way of masochistic fantasies or perversions, but she will then develop a great hostility toward men because of her anticipation of humiliation.

A man who feels deeply insecure in his masculinity easily suspects that he is accepted only because of the woman's need for sexual satisfaction, even though there may be evidence enough that she is genuinely fond of him; hence he will develop a resentment because of this feeling of being abused. Or a man may feel a lack of responsiveness from the woman as an unbearable humiliation, and thus be over-anxious that she find satisfaction. In his own eyes this great concern appears as considerateness. In other regards, however, he may be crude and inconsiderate, thus revealing that his concern for the woman's satisfaction is only his own protection against feeling humiliated.

There are two main ways of covering up the disparaging or defeating drives: covering them by an attitude of admiration, or intellectualizing them through skepticism. Skepticism may, of course, be the genuine expression of existing intellectual disagreements. It is only if such genuine doubts can be definitely excluded that one is justified in looking for hidden motivations. These may lie so close to the surface that simply questioning the validity of the doubts may provoke an attack of anxiety. One patient of mine disparaged me crudely at every interview, though without realizing that he did it. Later, when I merely asked him whether he really believed in his doubts concerning my competence in certain matters, he reacted by going into a state of severe anxiety.

The process is more complicated when the disparaging or defeating drives are covered by an attitude of admiration. Men who wish secretly to hurt and spurn women may in their conscious thoughts put them on a high pedestal. Women who unconsciously try always to defeat and humiliate men may be given to hero worship. In the hero worship of the neurotic, as in that of the normal person, there may be a genuine feeling for value and greatness, but the special characteristic of the neurotic's attitude lies in the fact that it is a compromise of two tendencies: blind adoration of success, regardless of its value, because of his own wishes in this direction; and a camouflage for his destructive wishes against a successful person.

Certain typical marriage conflicts are to be understood on this basis. In our culture the conflicts will more often concern women, because for men there are more external incitements to success and more possibilities of achieving it. Assume that a woman of the hero worshipping type marries a man because his existing or potential success appeals to her. Since in our culture a wife participates to some degree in her husband's success, this may give her some satisfaction, as long as the success lasts. But she is in a conflict situation: she loves her husband for his success and at the same time hates him for it; she wants to destroy it but is inhibited because on the other hand she wants to enjoy it vicariously by participating in it. Such a wife may betray her wish to destroy her husband's success by endangering his financial security through extravagance, by destroying his equanimity through enervating quarrels, by undermining his self-confidence through an insidious disparaging attitude. Or she may reveal her destructive wishes by relentlessly pushing him on to more and more success, with no regard for his own welfare. This resentment is likely to become more manifest at any sign of failure, and though during his success she may have appeared in all respects a loving wife she will now turn against her husband instead of helping and encouraging him, because the vindictiveness that was covered up as long as she could participate in his success emerges into the open as soon as he shows signs of defeat. All these destructive activities may go on under the camouflage of love and admiration.

Another familiar example may be cited to show how love is used to compensate the defeating drives arising from ambition. A woman has been self-reliant, capable and successful. After her marriage she not only gives up her work but develops an attitude of dependency and seems to give up ambition altogether—all of which

is preferably described as "becoming truly feminine."
The husband is usually disappointed, because he expected to find a good companion and instead he finds
himself with a wife who does not co-operate with him
but puts herself below him. A woman who undergoes
such a change has neurotic misgivings about her own
potentialities. She dimly feels that it will be safer to
achieve her ambitious goals—or even only security—
by marrying a man who is successful or in whom she at
least senses faculties for success. Thus far the situation need not call forth a disturbance, but may work
out satisfactorily. But the neurotic woman secretly objects to giving up her own ambition, feels hostile
toward her husband and, according to the neurotic all-
or-nothing principle, drops into feelings of nothingness
and eventually becomes a nonentity.

As I have said before, the reason that such a type
of reaction is more frequent in women than in men can
be found in our cultural situation, which stamps success a man's sphere. That this type of reaction is not
an inherent feminine trait is demonstrated by the fact
that men react in the same way if the situation is re-
versed, that is, if the woman happens to be stronger,
more intelligent, more successful. Because of our cultural belief in man's superiority in all but love, such an
attitude on the part of a man is less frequently disguised by admiration; it usually appears quite openly,
in a direct sabotage of the woman's interests and work.

The competitive spirit not only influences existing
relations between men and women, but even affects the
choice of a partner. In this regard what we see in neuroses is only a magnified picture of what is often normal in a competitive culture. Normally the choice of a
partner is often determined by strivings for prestige

or possession, that is, by motives lying outside the erotic sphere. In the neurotic person this determination may be all-prevailing, on the one hand because his strivings for dominance, for prestige, for support, are more compulsive and inflexible than in the average person, and on the other hand because his personal relations with others, including those of the opposite sex, are too deteriorated to enable him to make an adequate choice.

Destructive competitiveness may further homosexual tendencies in two ways: first, it supplies an impulse for one sex to withdraw from the other altogether so as to avoid sexual competition with equals; and second, the anxiety which it engenders calls for reassurance, and as pointed out before, the need for reassuring affection is often the reason for clinging to a partner of the same sex. This connection between destructive rivalry, anxiety and homosexual drives can often be observed in the process of analysis if patient and analyst are of the same sex. Such a patient may go through a period in which he boasts of his own achievements and disparages the analyst. At the beginning he does this in such disguised forms that he is not at all aware of doing it. Then he recognizes his attitude but it is still split off from his feelings, and he is not aware of how powerful an emotion is prompting it. Then, when he gradually starts to feel the impact of his hostility toward the analyst, and at the same time begins to feel increasingly uneasy—with anxiety dreams, palpitations, restlessness—he suddenly has a dream in which the analyst embraces him, and he becomes aware of fantasies and wishes for some close contact with the analyst, thus revealing his need to allay his anxiety.

This sequence of reactions may repeat itself several times before the patient eventually feels capable of facing the problem of his competitiveness as it is.

Thus, in short, admiration or love may serve as a compensation for the defeating drives as follows: by keeping the destructive impulses from awareness; by eliminating competitiveness altogether by creating an unsurpassable distance between self and competitor; by providing a vicarious enjoyment of success or participation in it; by propitiating the competitor and thus warding off his vindictiveness.

Though these remarks concerning the influence of neurotic competitiveness on sexual relations are far from exhaustive, they may suffice to show how it leads to an impairment of the relations between the sexes. This is all the more serious since the very competitiveness which in our culture undermines the possibility of attaining good relations between the sexes is also a source of anxiety and thus makes good relations all the more desirable.

· CHAPTER 12 ·

Recoiling from Competition

BECAUSE of its destructive character competitiveness in neurotic persons gives rise to a huge amount of anxiety, and consequently leads to a recoiling from competition. The question now is, Whence comes this anxiety?

It is understandable without any difficulty that one source is a fear of retaliation for the ruthless pursuit of ambition. One who steps on all others, humiliates and crushes them as soon as they have or want to have success, must have the fear that they will want just as intensely to defeat him. But such a retaliation fear, although it will be active in everyone who achieves success at the expense of others, is scarcely the whole reason for the neurotic's increased anxiety and his consequent inhibition toward competition.

Experience shows that retaliation fear alone does not necessarily lead to inhibitions. On the contrary, it may result merely in a cold-blooded reckoning with the imaginary or real envy, rivalry or malice of others, or in an attempt to expand one's power in order to be protected from any defeat. A certain type of successful person has only one goal, the acquisition of power and wealth. But if the structure of such personalities is compared with that of definitely neurotic persons there is one striking difference. The ruthless success-hunter does not care for the affection of others. He neither wants nor expects anything from others, neither help nor any kind of generosity. He knows that he can reach what he wants by his own strength and efforts alone. He will, of course, make use of people, but he cares for their good opinion only in so far as it is useful in attaining his own goal. Affection for its own sake means nothing to him. His desires and his defenses go along one straight line: power, prestige, possession. Even one who is driven to this kind of behavior by internal conflicts will not develop the usual neurotic characteristics if there is nothing within him to interfere with his strivings. Fear will only push him into enhanced efforts to be more successful and more invincible.

The neurotic person, however, pursues two ways that are incompatible: an aggressive striving for a "no one but I" dominance; and at the same time an excessive desire to be loved by everyone. This situation of being caught between ambition and affection is one of the central conflicts in neuroses. The main reason why the neurotic becomes afraid of his own ambitions and demands, why he does not even want to recognize them, and why he checks them or recoils from them altogether, is that he is afraid of losing affection. In other words, the reason why the neurotic checks his competitiveness is not that he has particularly stringent "super-ego demands" which prevent too great an aggressiveness, but that he finds himself caught in a dilemma between two equally imperative needs: his ambition and his need for affection.

The dilemma is practically unsolvable. One cannot step on people and be loved by them at the same time. Yet in the neurotic the pressure is so great that he does try to solve it. In general he attempts a solution in two ways: by justifying his drive for dominance and the grievances resulting from its nonfulfillment; and by checking his ambition. We can be brief about his efforts to justify his aggressive demands, because they have the same characteristics that we have already discussed in connection with the ways of obtaining affection and their justification. Here as there the justification is important as a strategy: it is attempted to make the demands incontestable so they will not block the way toward being loved. If he disparages others in order to humiliate them or crush them in a competitive fight, he will be deeply convinced that he is being wholly objective. If he wants to exploit others he will believe and try to make them believe that he is in great need of their help.

It is this need for justification that more than anything else allows an element of subtle underground insincerity to pervade a personality, even though the person may be basically honest. It accounts also for the relentless self-righteousness which is a frequent character trend in neurotic persons, sometimes conspicuous, sometimes hidden behind a complying or even self-recriminating attitude. This attitude of self-righteousness is often confounded with a "narcissistic" attitude. Factually it has nothing whatever to do with any kind of self-love; it does not even contain any element of complacency or conceit, because, contrary to appearances, there is never a real conviction of being right, but only a constant desperate need to appear justified. It is, in other words, a defensive attitude necessitated by the urge to solve certain problems which, in the last analysis, are generated by anxiety.

Observation of this need for justification was probably one of the factors that suggested to Freud the concept of the particularly severe "super-ego" demands which the neurotic submits to in reaction from his destructive drives. There is another aspect of the need for justification which is particularly suggestive of such an interpretation. In addition to being indispensable as a strategical means of dealing with others, justification is also in many neurotic persons a means of satisfying the necessity to appear irreproachable in their own eyes. I shall come back to this question when I discuss the role of guilt feelings in neuroses.

The direct outcome of the anxiety involved in neurotic competitiveness is a fear of failure and a fear of success. The fear of failure is in part an expression of the fear of being humiliated. Any failure becomes a catastrophe. A girl who had failed to know something she was expected to know at school not only felt inordinately ashamed, but felt also that the other girls in the class would despise and turn against her altogether. This reaction carries all the more weight since frequently occurrences are felt as failures which factually have no connotation of failure, or are at most immaterial—such as not getting the highest marks at school, or failing in some part of an examination, or giving a party which is not an extraordinary success, or not having been brilliant in conversation, in brief anything that falls short of excessive expectations. A rebuff of any kind, which, as we have seen, the neurotic reacts to with intense hostility, is likewise felt as a failure and therefore as a humiliation.

This fear of the neurotic person may be greatly intensified by his apprehension that others will gloat over a failure because they know of his relentless ambition. What he dreads more than failure itself is a failure after having shown in any way that he is competing, that he does indeed want success and has made efforts to attain it. He feels that a mere failure can be forgiven, might even arouse sympathy rather than hostility, but that once he has shown an interest in success he is surrounded by a horde of persecuting enemies, who lie in wait to crush him at any sign of weakness or failure.

The resulting attitudes vary according to the content of the fear. If the emphasis lies on the fear of failure as such, he will redouble his efforts or even become desperate in his attempts to avoid failure. Acute anxiety may emerge before crucial tests of his strength or ability, such as examinations or public appearances. If, however, the emphasis lies on the fear of others recognizing his ambition the resulting picture is exactly the opposite. The anxiety that he feels will make him appear to be disinterested and will lead him to make no efforts of any kind. The contrast in these two pictures is noteworthy, because it shows how two types of fear, which after all are akin, may produce two entirely different sets of characteristics. A person conforming to the first pattern will work frantically for examinations, but one of the second pattern will work very little and will perhaps conspicuously indulge in social activities or hobbies, thus showing to the world his lack of interest in the task.

Usually the neurotic is not aware of his anxiety and is conscious only of its consequences. He may, for example, be unable to concentrate on work. Or he may have hypochondriacal fears, such as a fear of heart trouble from physical exertion, or of a nervous breakdown from mental overwork. Or he may become exhausted after any exertion—when anxiety is involved in an activity it is likely to be exhausting—and will use this exhaustion to prove that efforts are injurious to his health and hence must be avoided.

In his recoil from making any effort the neurotic may lose himself in all sorts of diverting activities, from playing solitaire to giving parties, or he may take on an attitude that looks like laziness or indolence. A neurotic woman may dress badly, preferring to give the impression of not caring to dress well than to make the attempt to do so, because she feels the attempt would only expose her to ridicule. A girl who was unusually pretty, but was convinced that she was homely, did not dare to powder her nose in public because she expected people to think, "How ridiculous of that ugly duckling to make an attempt to look attractive!"

Thus in general the neurotic will consider it safer not to do the things he wants to do. His maxim is: Stay in the corner, be modest, and most of all, do not be conspicuous. As Veblen has emphasized, conspicuousness —conspicuous leisure, conspicuous consumption—plays an important role in competition. Accordingly a recoil from competition has to put emphasis on the opposite, on the avoidance of conspicuousness. This implies sticking to conventional standards, staying out of the limelight, being no different from others.

If this recoiling trend is a predominant characteristic it results in not taking any risks. Needless to say, such an attitude brings with it a great impoverishment in life and a warping of potentialities. For, unless circumstances are unusually favorable, the attainment of happiness or any kind of achievement presupposes taking risks and making efforts.

Thus far we have discussed the fear of possible failure. But this is only one manifestation of the anxiety involved in neurotic competitiveness. The anxiety may also take the form of a fear of success. In many neurotics anxiety concerning the hostility of others is so enormous that they are afraid of success, even if they feel certain of attaining it.

This fear of success results from fear of the begrudging envy of others and thus of the loss of their affection. Sometimes it is a conscious fear. A gifted writer among my patients renounced writing altogether because her mother began to write and proved to be successful. When after a long period she took it up again, hesitantly and apprehensively, she was afraid not of writing poorly but of writing too well. This woman was for a long time incapable of doing anything at all, the main reason being her excessive fear that others would begrudge her everything; instead she put all her energy into the task of making people like her. The fear may appear also as a mere vague apprehension that one would lose friends if one were to have any success.

In this fear, however, as in so many others, the neurotic person is more often aware not of his fear but only of the resulting inhibitions. When such a person plays tennis, for example, he may feel when he is close to victory that something holds him back and makes it impossible for him to win. Or he may forget to keep an appointment of decisive importance for his future. If he has something pertinent to contribute to a discussion or conversation he may speak in so low a voice, or in such condensed expression, that he will fail to make any impression. Or he will let others have the acclaim for work he has accomplished. He may observe that with some persons he can talk intelligently, while with others he is stupid; that with some he can play an instrument in a masterly fashion while with others he plays like a beginner. Although he feels bewildered by such an uneven state of affairs he is unable to change it. It is only when he has gained insight into his tendency to recoil that he will discover that when talking to a person less intelligent than himself he compulsively has to act still less intelligent; or that when playing with a poor musician he has to play still worse, driven by a fear that by excelling he would hurt and humiliate the other.

Finally, if he does have a success he is not only unable to enjoy it, but does not even feel it as his own experience. Or he will diminish it by attributing it to some fortuitous circumstances or to some insignificant stimulation or help from outside. After a success, however, he is likely to feel depressed, partly because of this fear, but also because of an unrecognized disappointment brought about by the fact that the actual success always remains far behind his secret excessive expectations.

Thus the conflict situation of the neurotic person derives from a frantic and compulsive wish to be the first in the race, and at the same time an equally great compulsion to check himself as soon as he gets well started or makes any progress. If he has done something successfully he is bound to do it poorly the next time. A good lesson is followed by a bad lesson, an improvement during treatment by a relapse, a good impression on people by a bad one. This sequence keeps recurring and gives him the feeling that he is waging a hopeless fight against overwhelming odds. He is like Penelope, who unravelled every night what she had woven during the day.

Thus inhibitions may set in at each step of the way: the neurotic may repress his ambitious wishes so completely that he does not even attempt a piece of work; he may try to do something but be unable to concentrate or carry it through; he may do excellent work but shrink from any evidence of success; and finally he may reach outstanding success and be unable to appreciate it or even feel it.

Among the many ways of thus recoiling from competition, perhaps the most important is that by which the neurotic creates in his imagination such a distance from his real or alleged competitor that any competition appears absurd, and is thereby eliminated in consciousness. This distance may be achieved either by setting the other person on a pedestal high out of reach, or by putting himself so far below all others that any competitive thoughts or attempts seem impossible and ridiculous. The latter process is what I shall discuss as "belittling."

Belittling oneself may be a conscious strategy, practiced merely for reasons of expediency. If the disciple of a great painter has done a good picture but has reason to fear the begrudging attitude of his master, he may belittle his work in order to allay the master's envy. The neurotic person, however, has only the vague notion of a tendency to undervalue himself. If he has done a good job he will seriously believe that others would have done better, or that his success was an accident and that he probably could not do so well again. Or, having done well, he may pick out some flaw, such as having worked too slowly, and use this to devaluate his entire accomplishment. A scientist may feel ignorant about questions concerning his own field, so that his friends have to remind him that he himself has written about them. When asked a question which is stupid or unanswerable he will be inclined to react with a feeling of his own stupidity; when reading a book with which he dimly disagrees he will be inclined, instead of thinking it through critically, to infer that he is too stupid to understand it. He may perhaps cherish the belief that he has managed to preserve a critical and objective attitude toward himself.

But not only will such a person take his inferiority feelings at their face value; he will insist on their validity. In spite of his complaints about them and the sufferings they cause him he is far from accepting any evidence to disprove them. If regarded as a highly competent worker he will maintain that he is being overvalued or that he has succeeded in bluffing others. The girl I mentioned heretofore, who developed an inordinate ambition at school after the humiliating experience with her brother, was always the first in her class and was regarded by everyone as a brilliant student, but was still convinced in her own mind that she was stupid. Although a glance into a mirror or the attention paid by men might be enough to convince a woman that she is attractive, she may still cling with an iron conviction to the belief that she is unattractive. A person may be convinced until he is forty that he is too young to assert his opinion or take a lead, and after forty he may switch to a feeling that he is too old. A well-known scholar was continually amazed at the reverence shown him, and in his own feelings insisted on being an insignificant mediocrity. Compliments are discarded as empty flattery or as prompted by ulterior motives, and may even result in anger.

Observations of this kind, which can be made almost without limit, show that inferiority feelings, perhaps the most common evil of our times, have an important function, and for that reason are maintained and defended. Their value consists in the fact that by lowering one's self in one's own mind and thereby putting one's self below other people and checking one's ambition, the anxiety connected with competitiveness is allayed.[1]

Incidentally it should not be overlooked that inferiority feelings may factually weaken one's position for the reason that self-belittling leads to an impairment of self-confidence. A certain amount of self-confidence is a prerequisite for any achievement, whether it be in varying a standard recipe for salad-dressing, selling merchandise, defending an opinion, or making a good impression on a potential relative.

A person with strong tendencies to belittle himself may have dreams in which his competitors excel, or in which he is at a disadvantage. Since there is no doubt that he subconsciously wishes for a triumph over competitors such dreams might look like a contradiction of Freud's contention that dreams represent wish fulfillments. Freud's view must not, however, be taken too

[1] D. H. Lawrence has given a striking description of this reaction in *The Rainbow* (p. 254). "This strange sense of cruelty and ugliness always imminent, ready to seize hold upon her, this feeling of the grudging power of the mob lying in wait for her, *who was the exception* [italics mine], formed one of the deepest influences of her life. Wherever she was, at school, among friends, in the street, in the train, she instinctively abated herself, made herself smaller, feigned to be less than she was, for fear that her undiscovered self should be seen, pounced upon, attacked by brutish resentment of the commonplace, the average Self."

narrowly. If direct wish-fulfillment involves too much anxiety, the allaying of that anxiety will be more important than a direct fulfillment of the wish. Thus when a person who is afraid of his ambition has dreams in which he is defeated, his dreams are the expression not of a wish to fail but of a preference for failure as the lesser evil. A patient of mine was scheduled to give a lecture during a period of her treatment when she was desperately fighting to defeat me. She had a dream that I was giving a successful lecture and that she was sitting in the audience, humbly admiring me. Again, an ambitious teacher dreamed that his pupil was the teacher and that he failed to know his assignment.

The degree to which self-belittling serves as a check on ambitions is shown also by the fact that the capacities that are belittled are usually the ones in which the individual desires most ardently to excel. If his ambition is of an intellectual character, intelligence is its instrument and hence is belittled. If his ambition is of an erotic character, appearance and charm are its instruments and hence they are belittled. This connection is so usual that one may guess from the focus of the self-belittling tendency where the greatest ambitions lie.

Thus far the feelings of inferiority have had nothing to do with any factual inferiority, but have been discussed only as the effects of a tendency to recoil from competition. Do they then have nothing to do with existing shortcomings, with a realization of actual flaws? They are in fact the result of both actual and imagined inadequacies: feelings of inferiority are a combination of anxiety-motivated belittling tendencies and a realization of existing defects. As I have emphasized sev-

eral times, we cannot ultimately fool ourselves, though
we may be successful in shutting certain impulses out
of awareness. And therefore a neurotic person of the
character we have been discussing will know, deep
down, that he has anti-social tendencies which he must
conceal, that he is far from genuine in his attitudes,
that his pretenses are quite different from the undercurrents below the surface. His registering of all these
discrepancies is an important cause for his feelings of
inferiority, even though he never recognizes clearly the
source of the discrepancies because they arise from repressed drives. Not recognizing their source, he gives
to himself reasons for feeling inferior which are rarely
the real reasons, but only a rationalization.

There is another reason why he feels that his inferiority feelings are the direct expression of an existing deficiency. On the basis of his ambitions he has
built up fantastic notions of his own value and importance. He cannot help measuring his realistic accomplishments against his notions of being a genius or a
perfect human being, and in this comparison his real
acts or his real possibilities appear inferior.

The total result of all these recoiling tendencies is
that the neurotic incurs real failures, or at most does
not get on as well as he should, considering his oppor-
tunities and his gifts. Others who started with him get
ahead of him, have better careers, greater success.
This lagging behind does not concern only external success. The older he becomes the more he feels the discrepancy between his potentialities and his achievements. He feels keenly that his gifts, whatever they
may be, are going to waste, that he is blocked in the
development of his personality, that he does not ma-

ture as time goes on.[2] And he reacts to the realization
of this discrepancy with a vague discontent, a discontent which is not masochistic but real and proportionate.

A discrepancy between potentialities and achievement may be due, as I have already pointed out, to external circumstances. But the discrepancy which develops in a neurotic person, and which is a never-failing
characteristic of neuroses, is due to his internal conflicts. His actual failures and the consequent increasing
discrepancy between potentialities and achievements
inevitably give even greater force to his existing inferiority feelings. Thus he not only believes himself to
be, but actually is inferior to what he might be. The impact of this development is all the greater since it puts
the inferiority feelings on a realistic basis.

Meanwhile the other discrepancy which I have mentioned—that between high-flown ambitions and the
comparatively poor reality—becomes so unbearable
that it demands a remedy. As such a remedy fantasy
offers itself. More and more the neurotic substitutes
grandiose ideas for attainable goals. The value they
have for him is obvious: they cover up his unendurable
feelings of nothingness; they allow him to feel important without entering into any competition and thus
without incurring the risk of failure or success; they
allow him to build up a fiction of grandeur far beyond
any attainable goal. It is this blind-alley value of grandiose fantasies that makes them dangerous, because

---

[2] C. G. Jung has clearly stated the problem of persons around the age of
forty becoming blocked in their development. But he has not recognized
the conditions leading up to such a situation, and therefore has not found
any satisfactory solution.

the blind alley has definite advantages for the neurotic when compared with the straightforward road.

These neurotic ideas of grandeur should be distinguished from those of the normal person and those of the psychotic. Even the normal person will at times think himself wonderful, attribute undue importance to what he is doing, or indulge in fantasies of what he might do. But these fantasies and ideas remain decorative arabesques and he does not take them too seriously. The psychotic person with ideas of grandeur is at the other end of the line. He is convinced that he is a genius, the Emperor of Japan, Napoleon, Christ, and will reject all evidence of reality which tends to disprove his conviction; he will be wholly unable to comprehend any reminder that he is actually a poor doorman or a patient in an asylum or the object of disrespect or ridicule. If he becomes aware of the discrepancy at all he will decide in favor of his grandiose ideas, and will believe that the others do not know any better, or that they are deliberately treating him with disrespect in order to hurt him.

The neurotic is somewhere between these two extremes. If he is at all aware of his exaggerated self-valuation his conscious reaction to it is rather like that of a healthy person. If in dreams he appears as royalty in disguise he may find such dreams funny. But his grandiose fantasies, although consciously he discards them as unreal, have for him an emotional reality-value similar to the value they have for a psychotic. In both cases the reason is the same: they have an important function. Although slender and shaky, they are the pillar on which his self-esteem rests, and therefore he has to cling to them.

The danger that lies in this function manifests itself in situations in which some blow is dealt the self-esteem. Then the pillar tumbles, he falls, and cannot recover from his fall. For example, a girl who had good reasons to believe that she was loved realized that the man was hesitating to marry her. In a talk he told her that he felt too young, too inexperienced to marry, and that he thought it wiser to know other girls before he tied himself definitely. She could not recover from this blow, became depressed, began to feel insecure in her work, developed an enormous fear of failure, with a subsequent desire to withdraw from everything, from people as well as from work. This fear was so overwhelming that even encouraging events, such as the man's later decision that he wished to marry her, and the offer of a better job with much flattering appreciation of her abilities, did not reassure her.

The neurotic, in contrast to the psychotic, cannot help registering with painful accuracy all the thousand little incidents of real life which do not fit in with his conscious illusion. Consequently he wavers in his self-valuation between feeling great and feeling worthless. At any minute he may shift from one extreme to the other. At the same time that he feels most convinced of his exceptional value he may be astonished that anyone takes him seriously. Or at the same time that he feels miserable and down-trodden he may feel furious that anyone should think him in need of help. His sensitivity can be compared with that of a person who is sore all over his body and flinches at the slightest touch. He easily feels hurt, despised, neglected, slighted, and reacts with proportionate vindictive resentment.

Here again we see a "vicious circle" at work. While

grandiose ideas have a definite reassurance value and afford some support, even though only in an imaginary way, they not only reinforce the tendency to recoil, but through the medium of sensitivity create greater rage and thereby greater anxiety. This is, to be sure, the picture of severe neuroses, but in minor degrees it can also be seen in less serious cases, where it may not even be recognized by the person concerned. On the other hand, however, a sort of lucky circle may start as soon as the neurotic is able to do some constructive work. By this means his self-confidence grows, and there is thus less necessity for his grandiose ideas.

The neurotic's lack of success—his falling behind others in any respect, whether it concern career or marriage, security or happiness—makes him envious of others and thus reinforces the attitude of begrudging envy which has developed from other sources. Several factors may lead him to repress his begrudging attitude, factors such as inherent nobility of character, a deep conviction that he has no right to demand anything for himself, or simply failure to recognize his existing unhappiness. But the more it is repressed the more it may be projected on others, resulting in a sometimes almost paranoid fear that others begrudge him everything. This anxiety may be so great that he feels positively uneasy if something good happens to him, a new job, a flattering recognition, a fortunate acquisition, good fortune in a love-relationship. Hence it may greatly reinforce his tendencies to refrain from having anything or getting anywhere.

Leaving out all details, the main outlines of the "vicious circle" which develops out of the neurotic striving for power, prestige and possession may be roughly indicated as follows: anxiety, hostility, impaired self-esteem; striving for power and the like; enhanced hostility and anxiety; tendency to recoil from competition (with accompanying tendencies toward self-belittling); failures and discrepancies between potentialities and achievements; enhanced superiority feelings (with begrudging envy); enhanced grandiose ideas (with fear of envy); enhanced sensitivity (with renewed tendency to recoil); enhanced hostility and anxiety, which starts the cycle all over again.

In order, however, to understand fully the role that envy plays in neuroses, we have to regard it from a more comprehensive viewpoint. The neurotic, whether or not he feels it consciously, is not only a very unhappy person indeed, but he does not see any chance of escaping his misery. What the outside observer describes as vicious circles developing out of attempts to get reassurance, the neurotic himself feels as being hopelessly caught in a net. As a patient of mine has described it, he feels caught in a cellar with many doors, and whichever door he opens leads only into new darkness. And all the time he knows that others are walking outside in sunshine. I do not believe that one can understand any severe neurosis without recognizing the paralyzing hopelessness which it contains. Some neurotic persons express their exasperation in no uncertain terms, but in others it is deeply covered by resignation or by a show of optimism. It may be difficult then to see that behind all the odd vanities, demands, hostilities, there is a human being who suffers, who feels forever excluded from all that makes life desirable, who knows that even if he gets what he wants he cannot enjoy it. When one recognizes the existence of all this hopelessness it should not be difficult to understand what appears to be an excessive aggressiveness or even meanness, unexplainable by the particular situation. A person so shut out from every possibility of happiness would have to be a veritable angel if he did not feel hatred toward a world he cannot belong to.

Coming back now to the problem of envy, this gradually developing hopelessness is the basis from which envy is constantly generated. It is not so much an envy of something special, but what Nietzsche has described as *Lebensneid,* a very general envy of everyone who feels more secure, more poised, more happy, more straightforward, more self-confident.

If such a feeling of hopelessness has developed in a person, regardless of whether it is close to his awareness or far away, he will attempt to account for it. He does not see it—as the analytical observer does—as the outcome of an inexorable process. Instead he sees it as caused either by others or by himself. Often he will blame both sources, though usually one or the other is in the foreground. When he puts the blame on others an accusatory attitude results, which may be directed toward fate in general, toward circumstances, or toward special persons: parents, teachers, husband, physician. Neurotic demands on others, as we have pointed out frequently, are to be understood largely from this point of view. It is as if the neurotic thought along these lines: "Since you are all responsible for my suffering, it is your duty to help me, and I have a right to expect it from you." In so far as he seeks the source of evil in himself, he feels that he has deserved his misery.

Speaking of the neurotic's tendency to put the blame

on others may give rise to a misunderstanding. It may sound as if his accusations were unwarranted. As a matter of fact he has definite good reasons to feel accusatory, because he has indeed been dealt with unfairly, particularly in childhood. But there are also neurotic elements in his accusations: they often take the place of constructive efforts toward positive goals and usually they are blind and indiscriminate. They may be directed, for example, toward persons who want to help him and at the same time he may be entirely incapable of feeling and expressing accusations against those persons who really injure him.

· CHAPTER 13 ·

Neurotic Guilt Feelings

In the manifest picture of neuroses guilt feelings seem to play a paramount role. In some neuroses these feelings are expressed openly and abundantly; in others they are more disguised but their presence is suggested by behavior, attitudes and ways of thinking and reacting. I shall discuss first in a summary description the various manifestations which indicate the existence of guilt feelings.

As I mentioned in the last chapter, a neurotic person is often inclined to account for his sufferings by feeling that he does not deserve any better. This feeling may be quite vague and indefinite, or it may be attached to thoughts or activities which are socially tabooed, such as masturbation, incest wishes, death wishes toward relatives. Such a person usually tends to feel guilty at the slightest occasion. If someone asks to see him his first reaction is to expect recrimination for something he has done. If friends do not come or write for some time he asks himself whether he has offended them. If anything goes wrong he assumes that it was his fault. Even if others are blatantly in the wrong, have definitely mistreated him, he still manages to blame himself for it. If there is any collision of interests or any argument he is inclined to assume blindly that the others are right.

There is but a fluctuating distinction between these latent guilt feelings, waiting to creep up on any occasion, and what has been interpreted as unconscious guilt feelings, evident in depressive conditions. The latter take the form of self-accusations that are often fantastic or at least grossly exaggerated. Also the neurotic's everlasting efforts to appear justified in his own and in others' eyes, particularly when the enormous strategical value of such efforts is not clearly recognized, suggest the existence of free-floating guilt feelings which have to be kept in abeyance.

The existence of diffuse guilt feelings is suggested further by the neurotic's haunting fear of being found out or of being disapproved of. In his discussions with the analyst he may act as if the relationship were that between criminal and judge, thus making it very difficult for him to be co-operative in the analysis. Every interpretation that is given him he will take as a reproach. If the analyst has shown him, for example, that there is a lurking anxiety behind a certain defensive attitude, he will answer, "I knew that I was a coward." If the analyst explains that he has not dared to approach people for fear of being rejected, he will take blame on his shoulders for having thus, as he interprets it, tried to make life easy for himself. The compulsive striving for perfection develops to a large extent out of this need to avoid any disapproval.

Finally, a neurotic person may feel definitely more at ease, even lose certain of his neurotic symptoms, if an adverse event occurs, such as losing a fortune or incurring an accident. Observation of this reaction, and also the fact that sometimes he seems to arrange or provoke adverse happenings, if only inadvertently, may lead to an assumption that the neurotic person has guilt feelings so strong that he develops a need for punishment in order to get rid of them.

Thus there seems to be a great deal of evidence not only for the existence of particularly keen guilt feelings in a neurotic person but also for the power they exert on his personality. But in spite of this apparent evidence it must be questioned whether the conscious guilt feelings of the neurotic person are really genuine and whether symptomatic attitudes suggestive of unconscious guilt feelings do not allow another interpretation. There are several factors which give rise to such doubts.

Guilt feelings, like inferiority feelings, are not at all unwelcome; the neurotic person is far from eager to get rid of them. In fact he insists on his guilt and vigorously resists every attempt to exonerate him. This attitude alone would suffice to indicate that behind his insistence on feeling guilty there must, as in inferiority feelings, be a tendency which has an important function.

And another factor should be kept in mind. It is painful to feel honestly regretful or ashamed of something, and more painful still to express the feeling to someone else; in fact a neurotic person, even more than others, will refrain from doing so, because of his fear of disapproval. What we have called guilt feelings, however, he expresses very readily.

Furthermore, the self-recriminations which are so frequently interpreted as indicating underlying guilt feelings in the neurotic are characterized by distinctly irrational elements. Not only in his specific self-

accusations, but also in his diffuse feelings of not de-
serving any kindliness, praise, success, he is likely to
go to any extreme of irrationality, from gross exag-
gerations to sheer fantasy.

Another factor suggesting that self-recriminations
are not necessarily the expression of genuine guilt
feelings is the fact that unconsciously the neurotic himself is not at all convinced of his unworthiness. Even
when he seems to be submerged in guilt feelings, he
may become very resentful if others show a tendency
to take his recriminations seriously.

The latter observation leads to a last factor, pointed
out by Freud when discussing self-accusations in melancholia:[1] the contradiction between the guilt feelings
that are manifested and the lack of that humility which
should accompany them. At the same time that he proclaims his unworthiness the neurotic will make great
demands for consideration and admiration and will
also show a distinct unwillingness to accept the slightest degree of criticism. This contradiction may be
glaringly obvious, as in the case of a woman who felt
vaguely guilty of every crime reported in the papers,
and even blamed herself for every death in the family,
but was so overwhelmed by an acute outbreak of rage
that she fainted when her sister rather mildly re-
proached her for requesting too much consideration.
But the contradiction is not always so conspicuous; it
is present much more frequently than appears on the
surface. The neurotic may mistake his self-accusatory
attitude for a sound critical attitude toward himself.

[1] Sigmund Freud, "Mourning and Melancholia" in *Collected Papers*,
vol. 4, pp. 152–170, Psychoanalytischer Verlag. Karl Abraham, *Versuch
einer Entwicklungsgeschichte der Libido*. Psychoanalytischer Verlag.

His sensitivity toward criticism may be screened by a belief that he can take criticism very well, if only it is made in a friendly or constructive manner; but this belief is only a screen and is contradicted by the facts. Even obviously friendly advice may be reacted to with anger, for advice of any kind implies criticism for not being altogether perfect.

Thus if guilt feelings are carefully examined and are tested for genuineness, it becomes apparent that much of what looks like feelings of guilt is the expression either of anxiety or of a defense against it. In part this holds true also for the normal individual. In our culture it is considered nobler to fear God than to fear men, or in non-religious terms, to refrain from something because of conscience rather than because of a fear of getting caught. Many a husband who pretends to be faithful because of his conscience is in reality merely afraid of his wife. Because of the great amount of anxiety in neuroses the neurotic is inclined more often than the normal individual to cover up anxiety with guilt feelings. Unlike the normal person he not only fears those consequences which are likely to happen, but anticipates consequences utterly disproportionate to reality. The nature of these anticipations depends on the situation. He may have an exaggerated notion of impending punishment, retaliation, desertion, or his fears may be completely vague. But whatever their nature his fears are all kindled at the same point, which may be roughly described as the fear of disapproval, or if the fear of disapproval amounts to a conviction, as a fear of being found out.

The fear of disapproval is very common in neuroses. Nearly every neurotic, even though he appear on surface observation to be entirely certain of himself and indifferent to the opinion of others, is excessively afraid of or hypersensitive to being disapproved of, criticized, accused, found out. As I have already mentioned, this fear of disapproval is usually understood to indicate underlying guilt feelings. In other words, it is considered to be a result of such feelings. Critical observation makes this conclusion questionable. In analysis a patient will often find it extremely difficult to talk about certain experiences or thoughts—those, for example, concerning death wishes, masturbation, incest wishes—because he feels so much guilt about them, or better because he believes he feels guilty. When he has gained sufficient confidence to talk about them, and recognizes that they do not meet with disapproval, the "guilt feelings" vanish. He feels guilty because, as a result of his anxieties, he is even more than others dependent on public opinion, and hence mistakes it naïvely as his own judgment. Furthermore his general sensitivity toward disapproval remains fundamentally unchanged, even if his special guilt feelings vanish after he has brought himself to talk about the experiences that prompted them. This observation suggests the conclusion that guilt feelings are not the cause but the result of the fear of disapproval.

Since the fear of disapproval is so important in both the development and the understanding of guilt feelings I shall interpolate here a discussion of some of its implications.

The disproportionate fear of disapproval may extend blindly to all human beings or it may extend only to friends—although usually the neurotic is unable to distinguish clearly between friends and enemies. In the beginning it refers only to the outside world, and to a greater or lesser extent it always remains related to the disapproval of others, but it may also become internalized. The more this happens, the more the disapproval from outside becomes unimportant in comparison with the disapproval of the self.

The fear of disapproval may appear in various forms. Sometimes it shows in a constant fear of annoying people; the neurotic may be afraid, for example, to refuse an invitation, disagree with an opinion, express any wishes, fail to conform to the given standards, be in any way conspicuous. It may appear in a constant fear of people finding out about him; even when he feels he is liked his inclination is to withdraw in order to forestall being found out and dropped. It also may come out in an inordinate reluctance to let others know anything about his own private affairs, or in a disproportionate anger at any harmless questions concerning himself, because he feels that such questions are attempts to pry into his affairs.

The fear of disapproval is one of the outstanding factors that makes the analytical process difficult for the analyst and painful for the patient. Different though each individual analysis is from the other, all have in common the feature that the patient, while desiring the analyst's help and while wishing to reach an understanding, must at the same time fight off the analyst as a most dangerous intruder. It is this fear that induces the patient to act as if he were a criminal before a judge, and, like the criminal, he is secretly grimly determined to deny and to mislead.

This attitude may appear in dreams of being pushed to confession and reacting to it with agony. One patient of mine, at a time when we were close to uncovering some of his repressed tendencies, had a day dream which was significant in this respect. He imagined he saw a boy who had the custom of finding refuge, every now and then, on a dream island. There the boy became part of a community governed by a law prohibiting any revelation of the island's existence and demanding the death of any possible intruder. A person whom the boy loved, and who represented the analyst in some disguised form, happened to find his way to the island. According to the law he should have been killed. The boy could save him, however, by pledging that he himself would never return to the island. This was an artistic expression of the conflict which from the beginning to the end of the analysis was present in one or another form, a conflict between liking the analyst and hating him because he wanted to intrude into hidden thoughts and feelings, a conflict between the patient's impulse to fight in defense of his secrets and the necessity of giving them up.

If the fear of disapproval is not generated by guilt feelings it may be asked why the neurotic is then so much concerned about being detected and disapproved of.

The main factor that accounts for the fear of disapproval is the great discrepancy that exists between the façade [2] which the neurotic shows both to the world and to himself and all the repressed tendencies that lie hidden behind the façade. Although he suffers, even more than he realizes, at not being at one with himself, at all the pretenses he must keep up, he has nevertheless to defend these pretenses with all his energy, because

[2] Corresponding to what C. G. Jung calls the "persona."

they represent the bulwark that protects him from his lurking anxiety. If we recognize that these things he has to hide form the basis of his fear of disapproval we can understand better why the disappearance of certain "guilt feelings" cannot possibly free him from his fear. There is more that has to be changed. To put it very bluntly, it is the whole insincerity in his personality or rather, in the neurotic part of his personality, that is responsible for his fear of disapproval, and it is in this insincerity that he fears detection.

As to the special content of his secrets, he wants in the first place to conceal the sum total of what is usually covered by the term aggression. This term is used to include not only his reactive hostility—anger, revenge, envy, desire to humiliate, and the like—but all his secret demands on others. Since I have already discussed these in detail it suffices here to say briefly that he does not want to stand on his own feet, that he does not want to make efforts of his own in order to achieve what he wants; instead he inwardly insists on feeding on other persons' lives, whether by domineering and exploiting or by the means of affection, "love" or submissiveness. As soon as his hostile reactions or his demands are touched upon, anxiety develops, not because he feels guilty but because he sees that his chances of getting the support he needs are endangered.

In the second place he wants to hide how weak and insecure and helpless he feels, how little he can assert himself, how much anxiety he has. For this reason he builds up a façade of strength. But the more his particular strivings for security are focussed on dominance, and thus the more his pride is also linked with the notion of strength, the more he thoroughly despises himself. He not only feels that there is danger in weakness but also considers it despicable, in himself as well as others, and he classes as weakness any inadequacy whether it concerns not being master in his own house, inability to overcome barriers within himself, having to accept help, or even being possessed by anxiety. Since he thus essentially despises any "weakness" in himself, and since he cannot help believing that others will despise him likewise if they find out his weaknesses, he makes desperate efforts to hide them, but always with the fear that he will be found out sooner or later; therefore the continued anxiety.

Thus guilt feelings and their accompanying self-recriminations are not only the result, instead of the cause, of a fear of disapproval, but they are also a defense against this fear. They fulfill the double purpose of inviting reassurance and of blurring the real issue. The latter purpose they accomplish either by diverting attention from what should be concealed, or by exaggerating so greatly that they appear untrue.

I shall cite two examples which may serve as illustrations of many. One day a patient accused himself bitterly of being ungrateful, of being a burden on the analyst, of not sufficiently appreciating the fact that the analyst treated him at a small fee. But at the end of the interview he found that he had forgotten to bring the money he had intended to pay that day. This was only one of many evidences of his wish to get everything for nothing. His profuse and generalized self-accusations had here as elsewhere the function of obscuring the concrete issue.

A mature and intelligent woman felt guilty about having had temper tantrums as a child, although she

knew, intellectually, that they had been provoked by
her parents' unreasonable conduct, and although in the
meantime she had freed herself of the belief that one
must think one's parents beyond reproach. Nevertheless her guilt feelings on this score persisted so
strongly that she was inclined to take her failure to
make erotic contacts with men as a punishment for her
hostility toward her parents. By blaming an infantile
offense for her present incapability of making such
contacts she disguised the factors factually operating,
such as her own hostility toward men and her having
withdrawn into a shell as a consequence of a fear of
rejection.

The self-recriminations not only protect against the
fear of disapproval but also invite positive reassurance, by provoking reassuring statements to the contrary. Even when no outside person is involved they
provide reassurance by enhancing the neurotic's self-
respect, for they imply that he has such a keen moral
judgment that he reproaches himself for faults which
others overlook and thus ultimately they make him feel
that he is really a wonderful person. Moreover they
give him relief, because they rarely concern the real
issue of his discontentment with himself, and therefore
factually leave a secret door open for a belief that he
is not so bad after all.

Before we proceed to discuss further functions of
self-recriminating tendencies we have to consider other
means of avoiding disapproval. A defense that is directly opposite to self-recrimination, and nevertheless
fulfills the same purpose, is forestalling any criticism
by always being right or perfect, thus leaving no vul-
nerable spots for criticism to find a foothold. Where

this type of defense prevails any behavior, even though glaringly wrong, will be justified with an amount of intellectual sophistry worthy of a clever and skillful lawyer. The attitude may go so far as to make it necessary to be right in the most insignificant and trifling details—to be always right about the weather, for example—because for such a person being wrong in any detail opens up the danger of being wrong altogether. Usually a person of this type is unable to endure the slightest difference of opinion, or even a difference of emotional emphasis, because in his thinking even a minute disagreement is equivalent to a criticism. Tendencies of this kind account to a great extent for what is called pseudo-adaptation. This is found in persons who in spite of a severe neurosis manage to maintain in their own eyes, and sometimes also in those of the people around them, an appearance of being "normal" and well adapted. In neurotics of this type one will scarcely ever go wrong in predicting an enormous fear of being found out or disapproved of.

A third way in which the neurotic may protect himself against disapproval is to take refuge in ignorance, illness or helplessness. I encountered a transparent example of this in a French girl whom I treated in Germany. She was one of the girls I have already mentioned who were sent to me under the suspicion of feeblemindedness. During the first few weeks of analysis I was doubtful myself about her mental capacity; she did not seem to understand anything I said, even though she understood German perfectly. I tried to say the same things in simpler language, with no better results. Finally two factors clarified the situation. She had dreams in which my office appeared as a jail, or as the office of a doctor who had examined her physically. Both ideas betrayed her anxiety at being found out, the latter dream because she was terrified of any physical examination. The other revealing factor was an incident in her conscious life. She had forgotten to present her passport at a certain time, as required by law. When at last she went to the official she pretended not to understand German, hoping in this way to escape punishment—an incident she related to me laughingly. She then recognized that she had been using the same tactics toward me, and for the same motives. From this time on she proved to be a very intelligent girl. She had been taking shelter behind ignorance and stupidity to escape the danger of being accused and punished.

In principle the same strategy is pursued by anyone who feels and acts like an irresponsible, playful child who is not to be taken seriously. Some neurotic persons adopt this attitude permanently. Or even if they do not behave childishly they may refuse to take themselves seriously in their own feelings. The function of this attitude may be observed in analysis. Patients on the verge of having to recognize their own aggressive tendencies may suddenly feel helpless, suddenly act like a child, desiring nothing but protection and affection. Or they may have dreams in which they find themselves small and helpless, carried in the mother's womb or in her arms.

If helplessness is not effective or applicable in a given situation, illness may serve the same purpose. That illness may serve as an escape from difficulties is well known. At the same time, however, it serves the neurotic as a screen against the realization that fear is making him recoil from tackling a situation as he should. A neurotic person who is having difficulties with his superior, for example, may find refuge in a severe attack of indigestion; the appeal of disability at such a time lies in the fact that it creates a definite impossibility of action, an alibi, so to speak, and thereby relieves him of the realization of his cowardice.[3]

A final and very important defense against disapproval of any kind is a feeling of being victimized. By feeling abused the neurotic wards off reproach for his own tendencies to take advantage of others; by feeling miserably neglected he debars reproaches for his tendencies toward possessiveness; by feeling that others are not helpful he prevents them from recognizing his tendencies to defeat them. This strategy of feeling victimized is so frequently used and tenaciously maintained because it is in fact the most effective method of defense. It enables the neurotic not only to ward off accusations but at the same time to put the blame on others.

To return now to self-recriminating attitudes, another function that they serve, in addition to protecting against a fear of disapproval and inviting positive reassurance, is to prevent the neurotic from seeing the necessity for change and in fact to serve as a substitute for change. To make any changes in a developed personality is extremely hard for everyone. But for the neu-

---

[3] If such a wish is interpreted—as Franz Alexander has done in *Psychoanalysis of the Total Personality*—as a need for punishment for having aggressive impulses against the superior, the patient will be very glad to accept such an explanation, because in this way the analyst helps him effectively to avoid facing the facts that it is necessary for him to assert himself, that he is afraid to do so, that he is irritable at himself for being afraid. The analyst allows the patient to feel backed up in his picture of himself as a person so noble that he is intensely bothered about any evil wishes against his superior, and thus reinforces his already present masochistic drives by lending them the glory of high moral standards.

rotic person this task is twice as hard, not only because
he has a greater difficulty in recognizing the necessity
for change, but also because so many of his attitudes
are necessitated by anxiety. Consequently he is mortally frightened at the prospect of having to change,
and he shrinks back from recognizing the necessity
for it. One of the means of shirking this knowledge is to
believe secretly that by self-recrimination he can "get
by." This process can frequently be observed in everyday life. If a person regrets having done something or
having failed to do it, and as a consequence wants to
make good or to change the attitude which was responsible, he will not submerge himself in guilt feelings. If he does do this it indicates that he shirks the
difficult task of changing. It is indeed so much easier
to be remorseful than to change.

Incidentally, another way in which the neurotic may
blind himself to the necessity for change is to intellec-
tualize his existing problems. Patients who are inclined to do this find a great intellectual satisfaction in
gaining psychological knowledge, including knowledge
concerning themselves, but let it remain at that. The
intellectualizing attitude is then used as a protection
which prevents them from experiencing anything emotionally, and thus from realizing that they would have
to change. It is as if they looked at themselves and
said: how interesting!

Self-recriminations may also serve to ward off the
danger of accusing others, for it may appear the safer
way to take guilt on one's own shoulders. Inhibitions
toward criticizing and accusing others, thus reinforcing
the tendencies to accuse one's self, play such a great
role in neuroses that they should be discussed at
greater length.

As a rule such inhibitions have a history. A child growing up in an atmosphere that creates fear and hatred and restrains his spontaneous self-esteem has deeply accusatory feelings against his surroundings. Not only, however, is he unable to express them, but if he is sufficiently intimidated he does not even dare to become aware of them in his conscious feelings. This is partly because of a simple fear of punishment, and partly because of his fear of losing the affection he requires. These infantile reactions have a solid basis in reality, inasmuch as parents who create such an atmosphere are scarcely ever able to take criticism, because of their own neurotic sensitivities. The ubiquity of this attitude that parents are infallible is due, however, to a cultural factor.[4] The position of parents in our culture is based on authoritative power which may always be relied on to enforce obedience. In many cases benevolence rules the relationships in the home, and there is no need for the parents to stress their authoritative power. Nevertheless as long as this cultural attitude exists it does somehow throw a shadow on the relationships, even when it remains in the background.

When a relationship is based on authority, criticism tends to be forbidden because it would undermine the authority. It may be openly forbidden and the ban be enforced by punishment, or, much more effectively, the prohibition may be more tacit and be enforced on moral grounds. Then the criticism of children is checked not only by the individual sensitivities of the parents, but also by the fact that the latter, pervaded by the cultural attitude that it is a sin to criticize parents, attempt implicitly and explicitly to influence the children to feel

[4] *Cf.* for this and the rest of the paragraph Erich Fromm's study in *Autoritaet und Familie,* ed. by Max Horkheimer (1936).

the same way. Under such conditions a less intimidated child may express some revolt, but in turn is made to feel guilty. A more intimidated child does not dare to show any resentment and gradually does not even venture to think that the parents may be wrong. He feels, however, that someone must be wrong, and thus comes to the conclusion that, since the parents are always right, it must be he who is at fault. Needless to say, this is usually not an intellectual but an emotional process. It is determined not by thinking but by fear.

In this way the child begins to feel guilty, or more accurately, he develops the tendency to seek and find fault within himself, instead of calmly weighing both sides and considering the whole situation objectively. His reproaches may lead him to feel inferior rather than guilty. There are only fluctuating distinctions between the two, depending entirely on the implicit or explicit emphasis on morals which is customary in his surroundings. A girl who is always subordinated to her sister and out of fear submits to the unjust treatment, choking the accusations she really feels, may tell herself that the unequal treatment is warranted because she is inferior to her sister (less beautiful, less brilliant), or she may believe it is justified because she is a bad girl. In both cases, however, she takes the blame on herself instead of realizing that she is being wronged.

This type of reaction does not necessarily persist; it may change if it is not too deeply ingrained, if the child's surroundings are changed, or if persons enter his life who appreciate him and emotionally support him. If such a change does not take place the inclination to transform accusations into self-accusations becomes

in time stronger rather than weaker. At the same time
that resentment against the world is gradually piling
up from several sources, the fear of expressing resentment is also growing, because of the increasing fear of
being found out and the assumption of the same sensitivity in others.

But recognition of the historical source of an attitude is not sufficient to explain it. Both practically and
dynamically the more important question is what factors carry the attitude at the time being. In the
neurotic's extraordinary difficulties in criticizing and
making accusations there are several determining factors in his adult personality.

In the first place this incapacity is one of the expressions of his lack of spontaneous self-assertion. In order
to understand this deficiency it is necessary only to
compare his attitude with the way the healthy person
of our culture feels and behaves in regard to making
and expressing accusations, or more generally speaking, in regard to attack and defense. The normal person is able to defend his opinion in an argument,
to refute an unwarranted accusation, insinuation or
imposition, to remonstrate internally or externally
against neglect or cheating, to refuse a request or an
offer if he does not like it and if the situation allows
him to refuse it. He is able to feel and express criticism if necessary, to feel and express accusations, or
deliberately to withdraw from or to dismiss a person
if he wants to. Furthermore he is able to defend or
attack without disproportionate emotional tension
and to hold a middle course between exaggerated
self-recriminations and an exaggerated aggressiveness
which would lead him to unwarranted, violent accusa-

tions against the world. To be able thus to take the happy medium is possible only on the basis of conditions which in neuroses are more or less lacking: a comparative freedom from diffuse unconscious hostility and a comparatively secure self-esteem.

When this spontaneous self-assertion is lacking the inevitable consequence is a feeling of weakness and defenselessness. A person who knows—perhaps without ever having thought about it—that if the situation demands it he can attack or can defend himself, is and feels strong. A person who registers the fact that he probably cannot do this is and feels weak. We register as accurately as an electric clock whether we have suppressed an argument out of fear or out of wisdom, whether we have accepted an accusation out of weakness or out of a sense of justice, even though we may successfully deceive our conscious selves. For the neurotic person this registering of weakness is a constant secret source of irritation. Many a depression starts after a person has been unable to defend his arguments or express a critical opinion.

A further important impediment to criticism and accusation is directly linked up with the basic anxiety. If the outside world is felt to be hostile, if one feels helpless toward it, then taking any risk of annoying people seems sheer recklessness. For the neurotic the danger appears all the greater, and the more his feeling of safety is based on the affection of others the more he is afraid of losing that affection. For him annoying another person has an entirely different connotation from what it has for the normal person. Since his own relations to others are thin and fragile he cannot believe that others' relations toward him are any better. Hence he feels that annoying them involves the danger of a final break; he expects to be dropped altogether, to be definitely spurned or hated. Besides, he assumes consciously or unconsciously that others are as much terrified as he is of being found out and criticized, and therefore he is inclined to treat them with as much delicacy as he would have them use toward him. His extreme fear of making or even feeling accusations puts him in a special dilemma because, as we have seen, he is filled with pent-up resentment. In fact, as everyone knows who is acquainted with neurotic behavior, plenty of accusations do find expression, sometimes in veiled, sometimes in open and most aggressive forms. Since I nevertheless assert that there is an essential meekness toward criticism and accusation it is worth while to discuss briefly the conditions under which such accusations will find expression.

They may be expressed under the stress of despair, more specifically, when the neurotic feels he has nothing to lose by it, when he feels that he will be rejected in any case, regardless of his behavior. Such an occasion arises, for example, if his special efforts to be kind and considerate are not returned right away or are rejected. Whether his accusations are discharged explosively in one scene, or whether they last for some time, depends on the duration of his despair. He may in a single crisis thrust upon others all he has ever held against them, or his accusations may extend over a longer period. He really means what he says, and expects the others to take it seriously—with the secret hope, however, that they will realize the depth of his despair and therefore condone him. Even with no despair a similar condition exists if the accusations concern persons whom the neurotic consciously hates and from whom he expects nothing good. In another condition, which we shall discuss presently, the very element of sincerity is missing.

The neurotic can also be accusatory with more or less vehemence if he feels that he is, or is in danger of being, found out and accused. The danger of upsetting others may then appear as the lesser evil compared to the danger of being disapproved of. He feels himself in an emergency and makes a counter-attack, like an animal which is apprehensive by nature and strikes out when in danger. Patients may thrust violent accusations upon the analyst at the time when they are most afraid of something being uncovered, or when they have done something for which they anticipate disapproval.

Unlike the accusations made under the stress of despair, attacks of this kind are made blindly. They are expressed without any conviction of being right about them, for they are born out of a sheer feeling of the need to ward off an immediate danger, regardless of what means are used. While they may incidentally contain reproaches which are felt to be real, in the main they are exaggerated and fantastic. Deep down the neurotic does not believe in them himself, does not expect them to be taken seriously and is greatly amazed if the other does so, if the other, for example, enters into a serious argument or shows signs of being hurt.

When we realize the fear of accusation that is inherent in the neurotic structure, and when we realize furthermore the ways in which this fear is dealt with, then we can understand why on the surface the picture is often contradictory in this respect. A neurotic person is often unable to express a warranted criticism, even though he is full of intense accusations. Every time he loses something he may be convinced that the maid has stolen it, but be quite unable to accuse her or even to object because she has not served dinner punctually. The accusations which he does express have often somehow a character of unreality, are not to the point, have a false coloring, are unwarranted or entirely fantastic. As a patient he may fling at the analyst wild accusations of ruining him, but be unable to express a sincere objection to the analyst's taste in cigarettes.

These open expressions of accusations are not usually sufficient to discharge all the pent-up resentment that is present. In order to do that indirect ways are necessary, ways which allow the neurotic to express his resentment without being aware that he does. Some of it comes out inadvertently, some is shifted from the persons he really means to accuse to comparatively indifferent persons—a woman may scold her maid, for example, when she has a grudge against her husband— or to circumstances or fate in general. These are safety valves which in themselves are not specific for neuroses. The specifically neurotic method for expressing accusations indirectly and unconsciously is to use the medium of suffering. By suffering the neurotic may present himself as a living reproach. A wife who becomes ill because her husband comes home late expresses her grudge more effectively than by making a scene, and also reaps the advantage of appearing in her own eyes as an innocent martyr.

How effectively suffering expresses accusations depends on the inhibitions toward raising accusations. Where the fear is not too intense, suffering may be demonstrated dramatically, with open reproaches of the general content, "Look how you have made me suffer." This in fact is a third condition under which accusations can be expressed, because suffering makes accusations appear warranted. There is also a close connection here with the methods used to obtain affection, which we have already discussed; accusatory suffering serves at the same time as a plea for getting pity and as an extortion of favors in reparation for harm done. The greater the restraint in making accusations the less demonstrative is the suffering. This may go so far that the neurotic will not even bring to the attention of others the fact that he is suffering. Altogether, we find the greatest variation in his demonstrations of his suffering.

Because of the fear that besets him on all sides the neurotic is constantly shuttling between accusations and self-recriminations. One result is a permanent and hopeless uncertainty as to whether or not he is right in criticizing or in considering himself wronged. He registers or knows by experience that very often his accusations are not warranted by reality but are provoked by his own irrational reactions. This knowledge too renders it difficult for him to recognize whether or not he is really wronged, and hence prevents him from taking a firm stand when necessary.

The observer is inclined to accept or interpret all these manifestations as expressions of particularly keen guilt feelings. This does not mean that the observer is neurotic, but it does imply that his as well as the neurotic's thinking and feeling are subject to cultural influences. To understand the cultural influences which determine our attitude toward guilt feelings we would have to consider historical, cultural and philosophical questions that would far surpass the scope of this book. But even in passing over the problem entirely it is necessary at least to mention the influence of Christian conceptions on questions of morals.

This discussion of guilt feelings can be very briefly summarized as follows. When a neurotic person accuses himself or indicates guilt feelings of some kind, the first question should be not "What is he really feeling guilty about?" but "What may be the functions of this self-recriminating attitude?" The main functions we have found are: expression for his fear of disapproval; a defense against this fear; and a defense against making accusations.

When Freud and with him the majority of analysts tend to consider guilt feelings as an ultimate motivation they reflect the thinking of their time. Freud recognizes that guilt feelings arise from fear, for he assumes that fear contributes to the generation of the "super-ego," which he makes responsible for guilt feelings; but he tends to believe that demands of conscience and feelings of guilt, once established, operate as an ultimate agency. Further analysis indicates that even after we have learned to react with guilt feelings to the pressure of conscience and accepted moral standards, the motivation behind these feelings—though it may show only in subtle and indirect ways—is a direct fear of consequences. If it is granted that guilt feelings are not in themselves the ultimate motivating power it becomes necessary to revise certain analytical theories which have been built up on the assumption that guilt feelings—particularly those of a diffuse character, which Freud tentatively called unconscious guilt feelings—are of paramount importance in bringing about the neurosis. I shall mention only the three most important of these theories: that of the "negative therapeutic reaction," which contends that the patient prefers to remain ill because of his unconscious guilt feelings; [5] that of the super-ego as an inner construction which inflicts punishments upon the self; and that of moral masochism, which explains self-inflicted suffering as the result of a need for punishment.

[5] *Cf.* K. Horney, "The Problem of the Negative Therapeutic Reaction" in *Psychoanalytic Quarterly*, vol. 5, 1936, pp. 29–45.

· CHAPTER 14 ·

The Meaning of Neurotic Suffering
(THE PROBLEM OF MASOCHISM)

WE HAVE seen that in struggling with his conflicts the neurotic person undergoes a great deal of suffering, that moreover he often uses suffering as a means of attaining certain goals which, because of existing dilemmas, are difficult to attain otherwise. Though we are able to recognize in every individual situation the reasons why suffering is used and the ends that are to be achieved by it, there remains some bewilderment why people should be willing to pay such an enormous price. It looks as if the generous use made of suffering, and the readiness to recoil from an active mastering of life, grow out of an underlying drive which can be roughly described as a tendency to make the self weaker instead of stronger, miserable instead of happy.

Since this tendency is contradictory to general conceptions of man's nature it has been a great puzzle, in fact a stumbling block to psychology and psychiatry. It is indeed the basic problem of masochism. The term masochism originally referred to sexual perversions and fantasies in which sexual satisfaction is obtained through suffering, through being beaten, tortured, raped, enslaved, humiliated. Freud has recognized that these sexual perversions and fantasies are akin to the general tendencies toward suffering, that is, those which have no apparent sexual foundations; these latter tendencies have been classified as "moral masochism." Since in sexual perversions and fantasies suffering aims at a positive satisfaction, the conclusion has been drawn that all neurotic suffering is determined by a wish for satisfaction, or to put it into simple language, that the neurotic wants to suffer. The difference between sexual perversions and so-called moral masochism is assumed to be a difference of awareness. In the former both the striving for satisfaction and the satisfaction are conscious; in the latter both are unconscious.

The obtaining of satisfaction through suffering is a big problem even in perversions, but it becomes still more puzzling in the general tendencies toward suffering.

Many attempts have been made to account for masochistic phenomena. The most brilliant of them is Freud's hypothesis of the death instinct.[1] This contends, briefly, that there are two main biological forces operating within man: the life instinct and the death instinct. The latter force, which aims at self-destruction, when combined with libidinal drives results in the phenomenon of masochism.

A question of great interest which I want to raise here is whether the tendency to suffer can be understood psychologically, without taking recourse to a biological hypothesis.

To begin with we have to tackle a misunderstanding, which consists in confounding actual suffering with the tendency to suffer. There is no warrant for jumping to the conclusion that since suffering exists there is

---

[1] Sigmund Freud, "Beyond the Pleasure Principle" in The International Psycho-Analytical Library No. 4.

therefore a tendency to incur it or even to enjoy it. For example we cannot, with H. Deutsch,[2] interpret the fact that in our culture women have pains in childbirth as a proof that women secretly enjoy these pains masochistically, even though this may certainly be true in exceptional cases. A great deal of the suffering that occurs in neuroses has nothing at all to do with a wish to suffer, but is only the unavoidable consequence of existing conflicts. It occurs just as pains occur after one has broken a leg. In both cases the pains appear regardless of whether the person wants them or not, and he does not gain anything by the suffering they incur. Manifest anxiety engendered by existing conflicts is the outstanding but not the only example for suffering of this type in neuroses. Other kinds of neurotic suffering are also to be understood in this way—such as the suffering which accompanies the realization of a growing discrepancy between potentialities and factual achievements, the feeling of being hopelessly caught in certain dilemmas, hypersensitivity to the slightest offenses, self-contempt for having a neurosis. This part of neurotic suffering, since it is quite unobtrusive, is often altogether neglected when the problem is tackled with the hypothesis that the neurotic wishes to suffer. And when this is done one wonders sometimes to what extent laymen and even some psychiatrists unconsciously share the contemptuous attitude which the neurotic himself has toward his neurosis.

Having eliminated the neurotic sufferings which are not caused by tendencies to suffer we turn now to those

[2] H. Deutsch, "Motherhood and Sexuality" in *Psychoanalytic Quarterly*, vol. 2 (1933), pp. 476–488.

which are so caused and hence fall under the category
of masochistic drives. In these the surface impression
is that the neurotic suffers more than is warranted by
reality. In more detail, he gives the impression that
something within him avidly seizes upon every opportunity to suffer, that he can manage to turn even fortuitous circumstances into something painful, that he
is quite unwilling to relinquish suffering. But here the
behavior which produces this impression is to a large
extent accounted for by the functions which neurotic
suffering has for the person concerned.

As to these functions of neurotic suffering I may
summarize what we have seen in the preceding chapters. Suffering may have a direct defense value for the
neurotic, and may often, in fact, be the only way he
can protect himself against imminent dangers. By self-
recrimination he avoids being accused and accusing
others, by appearing ill or ignorant he avoids reproaches, by belittling himself he avoids the danger of
competition—but the suffering he thereby brings on
himself is at the same time a defense.

Suffering is also a means of getting what he wants,
of carrying out his demands effectively and of putting
his demands on a justified basis. Concerning his wishes
toward life the neurotic is in a dilemma. His wishes
are, or have become, imperative and unconditional,
partly because they are prompted by anxiety, partly
because they are not checked by any real consideration
of others. But on the other hand his own capacity to
assert his demands is greatly impaired, because of his
lack of spontaneous self-assertion, in more general
terms because of his basic feeling of helplessness. The
result of this dilemma is that he expects others to take

care of his wishes. He gives the impression that underlying his actions is a conviction that others are responsible for his life and that they are to be blamed if things go wrong. This collides with his conviction that no one grants him anything, and the result is that he feels he has to coerce others to fulfill his wishes. It is here that suffering comes to his assistance. Suffering and helplessness become his outstanding means of obtaining affection, help, control, and at the same time allow him to evade all demands that others might make on him.

Suffering has finally the function of expressing accusations against others in a disguised but effective way. It is this that we have discussed in some detail in the preceding chapter.

When the functions of neurotic suffering are recognized the problem is divested of some of its mysterious character, but is still not completely solved. In spite of the strategical value of suffering there is one factor which lends support to the notion that the neurotic wants to suffer: often he suffers more than is warranted by the strategical goal, tends to exaggerate his misery, to submerge himself in feelings of helplessness, unhappiness and unworthiness. Even though we know that his emotions are likely to be exaggerated and that they cannot be taken at face value, we are struck by the fact that the disappointments which result from his conflicting tendencies throw him into an abyss of misery which is disproportionate to the significance that the situation had for him. When he has been but moderately successful he dramatically exaggerates his defeat as an irrevocable disgrace. When he has merely failed to assert himself his self-esteem drops like a deflated balloon. When during analysis he has to face the unpleasant prospect of working through a new problem he drops into absolute hopelessness. We still have to examine why he thus seemingly voluntarily increases his suffering beyond the strategical necessities.

In such suffering there are no apparent advantages to be gained, no audience that might be impressed, no sympathy to be won, no secret triumph in asserting his will over others. Nevertheless, there is a gain for the neurotic, but of a different kind. Incurring a failure in love, a defeat in competition, having to realize a definite weakness or shortcoming of his own is unbearable for one who has such high-flown notions of his uniqueness. Thus when he dwindles to nothing in his own estimation, the categories of success and failure, superiority and inferiority cease to exist; by exaggerating his pain, by losing himself in a general feeling of misery or unworthiness, the aggravating experience loses some of its reality, the sting of the special pain is lulled, narcotized. The principle operating in this process is a dialectic one, containing the philosophical truth that at a certain point quantity is converted into quality. Concretely, it means that though suffering is painful, abandoning one's self to excessive suffering may serve as an opiate against pain.

A masterly description of this process is given in a Danish novel.[3] The story concerns a writer whose beloved wife had been lust-murdered two years before. He had been warding off the unbearable pain by only dimly experiencing what had happened. To escape the

[3] Aage von Kohl, *Der Weg durch die Nacht* (translated from Danish into German).

realization of his grief he had plunged into work and had written a book, working day and night. The narrative begins the day the book is finished, that is, at the psychological moment when he would have to face his pain. We meet him first at the cemetery, whither his steps have inadvertently led him. We see him indulging in the most gruesome and fantastic speculations on such thoughts as worms eating the dead, people buried alive. He is exhausted and returns home, where his torture continues. He is impelled to recall minutely what had happened. Perhaps the murder would not have occurred if he had gone with his wife that evening when she visited friends, if she had reached him by telephone to ask him to call for her, if she had stayed with the friends, if he had taken a walk and happened to meet her at the station. Impelled to imagine in detail how the murder took place he becomes submerged in an ecstasy of pain, until finally he loses consciousness. Thus far the story is of particular interest for the problem we have been discussing. What happens further is that after having recovered from his orgy of torment he still has to work through the problem of taking revenge, and ultimately he becomes capable of facing his pain realistically. The process that is presented in this story is the same that can be seen in certain mourning customs that serve to alleviate the pain of loss by acutely intensifying it and inducing complete abandonment to it.

When this narcotic effect of exaggerated pain is recognized we have a further help in finding understandable motivations in masochistic drives. But there still remains the question of why such suffering can yield satisfaction, as it obviously does in masochistic perversions and fantasies and as we suspect it does in the general neurotic tendencies toward suffering.

In order to be able to answer this question it is necessary to recognize first the elements which all masochistic tendencies have in common, or more accurately, the basic attitude toward life that underlies such tendencies. When they are examined from this point of view the common denominator is definitely found to be a feeling of intrinsic weakness. This feeling appears in the attitude toward the self, toward others, toward fate in general. Briefly it can be described as a deep feeling of insignificance or rather of nothingness; a feeling of being like a reed that can easily be swayed by any wind; a feeling of being in the power of others, of being at their beck and call, appearing in a tendency toward over-compliance and in a defensive over-emphasis on control and not giving in; dependence on affection and the judgment of others, the first showing in an inordinate need for affection, the latter in an inordinate fear of disapproval; a feeling of not having a say in one's own life but of having to let others bear the responsibility for it and make the decisions; a feeling that good and evil come from outside, that one is entirely helpless toward fate, appearing negatively in a sense of impending doom, positively in an expectation of some miracle happening without one's moving a finger; a feeling toward life in general that one cannot breathe, work, enjoy anything without others supplying the incentive, the means and the aims; a feeling of being putty in the master's hands. How are we to understand this feeling of intrinsic weakness? Is it in the last analysis the expression of a lack of vital strength? It may be this in some cases, but on the whole differences in vitality among neurotics are in no way greater than in other people. Is it a simple consequence of the basic anxiety? Certainly anxiety has something to do with it, but anxiety alone may have the opposite effect of impelling one to strive for and attain more and more strength and power in order to be safe.

The answer is that primarily this feeling of intrinsic weakness is not a fact at all; what is felt as weakness and appears as weakness is only the result of an inclination toward weakness. This fact can be recognized from characteristics we have already discussed: in his own feelings the neurotic unconsciously exaggerates his weakness and he tenaciously insists on being weak. It is, however, not only by logical deduction that this inclination toward weakness can be discovered; very often it can be seen at work. Patients may imaginatively seize upon every possibility of believing that they have an organic illness. One patient, whenever any difficulty arose, quite consciously wished to have tuberculosis, lie in a sanitarium and be completely taken care of. If any demand is made such a person's first impulse may be to yield, and he will then go to the other extreme and refuse to give in at any price. In analysis a patient's self-recriminations are often the result of his adopting as his own opinion an anticipated criticism, thus showing his readiness to surrender in advance to any judgment. The tendency blindly to accept authoritative statements, to lean on someone, always to recoil from a difficulty with a helpless "I can't" instead of accepting it as a challenge, is a further evidence of the inclination toward weakness.

Usually the sufferings entailed in these tendencies toward weakness yield no conscious satisfaction but, on the contrary, regardless of the purpose they serve, are definitely part of the neurotic's general awareness of misery. Nevertheless these tendencies aim at a satisfaction, even when they do not, or at least apparently do not, reach it. Occasionally this aim can be observed and sometimes it even becomes apparent that the goal of satisfaction has been achieved. A patient who went to visit some friends living in the country felt disappointed that no one met her at the station and that some of the friends were not at home when she arrived. Thus far, she said, the experience was wholly painful. But then she felt herself sliding into a feeling of being utterly desolate and forlorn, a feeling which, soon afterwards, she recognized as entirely disproportionate to the provocation. This submergence in misery not only lulled the pain but was felt as positively pleasurable.

The achievement of satisfaction is much more frequent and more obvious in sexual fantasies and perversions of a masochistic character, such as fantasies of being raped, beaten, humiliated, enslaved, or their actual enactment. In fact they are only another manifestation of this same general inclination toward weakness.

The obtaining of satisfaction by submersion in misery is an expression of the general principle of finding satisfaction by losing the self in something greater, by dissolving the individuality, by getting rid of the self with its doubts, conflicts, pains, limitations and isolation.[4] This is what Nietzsche has called liberation from

---

[4] This interpretation of the kind of satisfaction attained in masochism is basically the same as that of E. Fromm, *op. cit.*, ed. by Max Horkheimer (1936).

the *principium individuationis*. It is what he means by the "dionysian" tendency and he considers it one of the basic strivings in human beings, as opposed to what he calls the Apollonian tendency, which works toward an active molding and mastering of life. Ruth Benedict speaks of dionysian trends in referring to attempts to induce ecstatic experience, and has pointed out how widespread these tendencies are among the various cultures, and how manifold their expressions.

The term "dionysian" is taken from the Dionysos cults in Greece. These, as well as the earlier cults of the Thracians,[5] had as their aim the extreme stimulation of all feelings up to visionary states. The means of producing ecstatic states were music, uniform rhythm of flutes, raving dances at night, intoxicating drinks, sexual abandon, all working up to a seething excitement and ecstasy. (The term ecstasy means literally being outside or beside oneself.) All over the world there are customs and cults following the same principle: in groups abandonment in festivals and religious ecstasy, and in individuals, oblivion in drugs. Pain also plays a role in producing the dionysian condition. In some Plains Indian tribes visions are induced by fasting, cutting off a piece of flesh, being tied in a painful position. In the Sun Dances, one of the most important ceremonies of the Plains Indians, physical torture was a very common means of stimulating ecstatic experiences.[6] The Flagellantes in the Middle Ages used beatings to produce ecstasy. the Penitentes

---

[5] Erwin Rohde, *Psyche*, the cult of souls and belief in immortality among the Greeks (1925).

[6] Leslie Spier, "The Sun Dance of the Plains Indians: Its Development and Diffusion" in *Anthropological Papers of the American Museum of Natural History*, vol. 16, part 7 (New York 1921).

in New Mexico used thorns, beatings, the carrying of heavy loads.

Though these cultural expressions of dionysian tendencies are far from being patterned experiences in our culture, they are not entirely alien to us. To some degree all of us know the satisfaction derived from "losing ourselves." We feel it in the process of falling asleep after a physical or mental strain or of going into a narcosis. The same effect can be induced by alcohol. In the use of alcohol certainly losing inhibitions is one of the factors involved, and lulling grief and anxiety is another, but here too the ultimate satisfaction aimed at is the satisfaction of oblivion and abandon. And there are few persons who do not know the satisfaction of losing themselves in some great feeling, whether it be love, nature, music, enthusiasm for a cause, or sexual abandon. How can we account for the apparent universality of these strivings?

In spite of all the happiness life can afford, it is at the same time full of inescapable tragedy. Even if there is no particular suffering, there still remain the facts of old age, sickness and death; in still more general terms, the fact remains inherent in human life that the individual is limited and isolated—limited in what he can understand, achieve or enjoy, isolated because he is a unique entity, separate from his fellow beings and from surrounding nature. In fact, it is this individual limitation and isolation which most of the cultural trends toward oblivion and abandon tend to overcome. The most poignant and beautiful expression of this striving is found in the Upanishad, in the picture of rivers which flow and, disappearing into the ocean, lose name and shape. By dissolving the self in something greater, by becoming part of a greater entity, the individual overcomes to a certain extent his limitations; as it is expressed in the Upanishad, "By vanishing to nothing, we become part of the creative principle of the universe." This seems to be the great consolation and gratification which religion has to offer human beings; by losing themselves they can become at one with God or nature. The same satisfaction can be achieved by devotion to a great cause; by surrendering the self to a cause we feel at one with a greater whole.

In our culture we are more aware of the opposite attitude toward the self, the attitude that emphasizes and highly values the particularities and uniqueness of individuality. Man in our culture feels strongly that his own self is a separate unity, distinguished from or opposite to the world outside. Not only does he insist on this individuality but he derives a great deal of satisfaction from it; he finds happiness in developing his special potentialities, mastering himself and the world in active conquest, being constructive and doing creative work. Of this ideal of personal development Goethe has said, "*Hoechstes Glueck der Menschenkinder ist doch die Persoenlichkeit.*"

But the opposite tendency that we have discussed—the tendency to break through the shell of individuality and be rid of its limitations and isolation—is an equally deep-rooted human attitude, and is also pregnant with potential satisfaction. Neither of these tendencies is in itself pathological; both the preservation and development of individuality and the sacrifice of individuality are legitimate goals in the solution of human problems.

There is scarcely any neurosis in which the tendency to get rid of the self does not appear in a direct form.

It may appear in fantasies of leaving home and becoming a derelict or of losing one's identity; in an identification with a person one is reading about; in a feeling,
as one patient has put it, of being forlorn amid the
darkness and the waves, of being at one with the darkness and the waves. The tendency is present in wishes
to be hypnotized, in an inclination toward mysticism, in
feelings of unreality, in an inordinate need for sleep,
in the lure of sickness, insanity, death. And as I have
mentioned before, in masochistic fantasies the common
denominator is a feeling of being putty in the master's
hand, of being devoid of all will, of all power, of being
absolutely subjected to another's domination. Each different manifestation is of course determined in its special way and has its own implication. A feeling of being
enslaved, for example, may be part of a general tendency to feel victimized, and as such be a defense against
impulses to enslave others and also an accusation
against others for not letting themselves be dominated.
But while it has this value of expressing defense and
hostility, it has also the secret positive value of self-
surrender.

Whether the neurotic subjects himself to a person or
to fate, and whatever the kind of suffering which he
allows to overpower him, the satisfaction he seeks
seems to be the weakening or extinction of his individual self. He ceases then to be the active carrier of actions and becomes an object, without a will of his own.

When masochistic strivings are thus integrated into
the general phenomenon of a striving to relinquish the
individual self, the satisfaction that is sought or attained by weakness and suffering loses its strangeness;

it is put in a frame of reference that is familiar. [7] The tenaciousness of masochistic strivings in neurotics is then accounted for by the fact that at the same time they serve as a protection against anxiety and provide a potential or real satisfaction. As we have seen, this satisfaction is seldom real except in sexual fantasies or perversions, even though the striving for it is an important element in the general tendencies toward weakness and passivity. Thus a final question arises as to why the neurotic so rarely attains the oblivion and abandon, and thus the satisfaction, which he seeks.

An important circumstance which prevents a definite satisfaction is that the masochistic drives are counteracted by the neurotic's extreme emphasis on the uniqueness of his individuality. Most masochistic phenomena share with neurotic symptoms the character of being a compromise solution of incompatible strivings. The neurotic tends to feel a prey to everyone's will, but at the same time insists that the world should adapt itself to him. He tends to feel enslaved, but at the same time insists that his power over others should be unquestioned. He wants to be helpless and taken care of, but at the same time insists on being not only entirely self-sufficient but, in effect, omnipotent. He tends to feel that he is nothing, but is irritated when he is not taken for a genius. There is absolutely no satisfactory solution which could reconcile such extremes, particularly since both strivings are so strong.

[7] W. Reich in "Psychisches Korrelat und vegetative Stroemung" and in "Ueber Charakteranalyse" has made a similar attempt at a solution of the problem of masochism. He too contends that masochistic tendencies are not opposed to the pleasure principle. He puts them, however, on a sexual basis, and what I have described as the striving for a dissolution of individual boundaries he conceives as a striving for orgasm.

The drive toward oblivion is much more imperative in the neurotic than in the normal person because the former wants to get rid not only of the fears, limitations and isolations that are universal in human existence, but also of a feeling that he is trapped in insoluble conflicts and their resultant sufferings. And his contradictory drive toward power and self-aggrandizement is equally imperative and more than normally intense. Of course he does attempt to achieve the impossible, to be at once everything and nothing; he may, for example, live in a helpless dependence and at the same time exert a tyranny over others by means of his weakness. Such compromises he may himself mistake as a capacity for surrender. In fact, sometimes even psychologists seem inclined to confound the two, and to assume that surrender is in itself a masochistic attitude. In reality the masochistic person is, on the contrary, entirely incapable of giving himself to anything or anyone; he is incapable, for example, of putting all his energies into the service of a cause, or of wholly giving himself in love to another person. He can surrender himself to suffering but in this surrender he is wholly passive, and the feeling or the interest or the person which is the cause of his suffering he uses only as a means to lose himself for the sake of losing himself. There is no active interplay between himself and the other, but only his self-centered absorption in his own ends. Genuine surrender to a person or a cause is a manifestation of inner strength; masochistic surrender is ultimately a manifestation of weakness.

Another reason why the satisfaction that is sought is seldom attained lies in the destructive elements inherent in the neurotic structure I have described. These are missing in the cultural "dionysian" drives. In the latter there is nothing comparable to the neurotic destructiveness of all that constitutes the personality, of all its potentialities for achievement and happiness. Let us compare the Greek dionysian cult with, for example, the neurotic fantasies of becoming insane. In the former the desire was for a transitory ecstatic experience serving to enhance the joy of life; in the latter the same drive toward oblivion and abandon serves neither as a temporary submergence leading to re-emergence, nor as a means of making life richer and fuller. Its goal is to get rid of the whole tormenting self, regardless of its values, and therefore the intact part of the personality reacts to it with fear. In fact, fear of the disastrous possibilities toward which part of the personality impels the whole is usually the only factor in the process that impinges upon awareness. All the neurotic knows about it is that he has a fear of becoming insane. Only when the process is separated into its component parts—a drive toward self-relinquishment and a reactive fear—can it be understood that he is striving for a definite satisfaction but is prevented by his fears from attaining it.

One factor peculiar to our culture serves to reinforce the anxiety connected with the drives toward oblivion. In Western civilization there are but few, if any, cultural patterns in which these drives, even regardless of their neurotic character, can be satisfied. Religion, which offered such a possibility, has lost its power and appeal for the majority. Not only are there no effective cultural means for such satisfaction, but their development is actively discouraged, for in an individualistic culture the individual is expected to stand on his own feet, assert himself, and if necessary fight his way. In our culture to yield realistically to tendencies toward self-relinquishment involves the danger of ostracism.

In view of the fears that usually debar the neurotic from the specific satisfactions for which he is striving, it is possible to understand the value for him of masochistic fantasies and perversions. If his drives for self-relinquishment are lived out in fantasies or in sexual practices he can perhaps escape his danger of complete self-obliteration. Like the dionysian cults, these masochistic practices provide a temporary oblivion and abandon, with comparatively little risk of harm to the self. Usually they pervade the whole structure of the personality; sometimes they are concentrated on sexual activities, while other parts of the personality remain comparatively free of them. There are men who are able to be active, aggressive and successful in their own work, but are impelled from time to time to indulge in masochistic perversions such as dressing like a woman or playing the naughty boy and having themselves beaten. On the other hand, the fears that prevent the neurotic from finding a satisfactory solution of his difficulties may also pervade his masochistic drives. If these drives are of a sexual nature he will then, in spite of intense masochistic fantasies concerning sexual relations, keep away from sexuality altogether, showing a repugnance toward the other sex, or at least grave sexual inhibitions.

Freud regards masochistic drives as an essentially sexual phenomenon. He has propounded theories to account for them. Originally he regarded masochism as an aspect of a definite, biologically determined stage of sexual development, the so-called anal-sadistic stage.

Later he added the hypothesis that masochistic drives have an inherent kinship with feminine nature and imply something like living out a wish to be a woman. [8] His last assumption, as mentioned before, is that masochistic drives are a combination of self-destructive and sexual drives, and that their function is to render the self-destructive drives harmless to the individual.

My point of view, on the other hand, may be summed up as follows. Masochistic drives are neither an essentially sexual phenomenon nor the result of biologically determined processes, but originate in personality conflicts. Their aim is not suffering; the neurotic wishes to suffer as little as anyone else wishes it. Neurotic suffering, inasmuch as it serves certain functions, is not what the person wants but what he pays, and the satisfaction he aims at is not suffering itself but a relinquishment of the self.

[8] S. Freud, "The Economic Principle of Masochism" in *Collected Papers*, vol. 2, pp. 255–268, and *New Introductory Lectures on Psychoanalysis*. See also Karen Horney, "The Problem of Feminine Masochism" in *Psychoanalytic Review*, vol. 22 (1935).

· CHAPTER 15 ·

Culture and Neurosis

EACH individual analysis offers new problems even to the most experienced analyst. In each patient he finds himself confronted with difficulties he has never encountered before, with attitudes which are hard to recognize and still harder to explain, with reactions which are far from transparent at first sight. Looking back at the intricacy of the neurotic character structure, as described in the preceding chapters, and at the many factors involved, this variety is not surprising. Differences in inheritance and in the experiences a person has gone through during his life, particularly in his childhood, produce a seemingly boundless variation in the construction of the factors involved.

But, as pointed out at the beginning, in spite of all these individual variations the crucial conflicts around which a neurosis grows are practically always the same. In general they are the same conflicts to which the healthy person in our culture is also subject. It is something of a truism to say that it is impossible to distinguish clearly between neurotic and normal, but it may be useful to repeat it once more. Many readers, confronted by conflicts and attitudes that they recognize in their own experience, may ask themselves: Am I neurotic or not? The most valid criterion is whether or not the individual feels handicapped by his conflicts, whether he can face them and deal with them directly.

When we have recognized that neurotic persons in our culture are impelled by the same underlying conflicts, and that in a diminished degree the normal person is also subject to them, we are confronted again with the question that was raised at the beginning: what are the conditions in our culture which are responsible for the fact that neuroses center around these particular conflicts I have described, and not others?

Freud has given this problem but limited consideration; the reverse side of his biological orientation is a lack of sociological orientation, and thus he tends to attribute social phenomena primarily to psychic factors and these primarily to biological factors (libido theory). This tendency has led psychoanalytical writers to believe, for example, that wars are caused by the working of the death instinct, that our present economic system is rooted in anal-erotic drives, that the reason the machine age did not start two thousand years ago is to be found in the narcissism of that period.

Freud sees a culture not as the result of a complex social process but primarily as the product of biological drives which are repressed or sublimated, with the result that reaction formations are built up against them. The more complete the suppression of these drives, the higher the cultural development. Since the capacity for sublimation is limited and since the intensive suppression of primitive drives without sublimation may lead to neurosis, the growth of civilization must inevitably imply a growth of neurosis. Neuroses are the price humanity has to pay for cultural development.

The implicit theoretical presupposition underlying this train of thought is a belief in the existence of biologically determined human nature, or more precisely, a belief that oral, anal, genital and aggressive drives exist in all human beings in approximately equal quantities. Variations in character formation from individual to individual, as from culture to culture, are due, then, to the varying intensity of the suppression required, with the additional qualification that this suppression affects the different kinds of drives in varying degrees.

Historical and anthropological findings do not confirm such a direct relation between height of culture and the suppression of sexual or aggressive drives. The error consists primarily in assuming a quantitative instead of a qualitative relation. The relation is not between quantity of suppression and quantity of culture but between quality of individual conflicts and quality of cultural difficulties. The quantitative factor cannot be disregarded, but it can be evaluated only in the context of the entire structure.

There are certain typical difficulties inherent in our culture, which mirror themselves as conflicts in every individual's life and which, accumulated, may lead to the formation of neuroses. Since I am not a sociologist I shall merely point out briefly the main trends which have a bearing on the problem of neurosis and culture.

Modern culture is economically based on the principle of individual competition. The isolated individual has to fight with other individuals of the same group, has to surpass them and, frequently, thrust them aside. The advantage of the one is frequently the disadvantage of the other. The psychic result of this situation is a diffuse hostile tension between individuals. Everyone is the real or potential competitor of everyone else. This situation is clearly apparent among members of the same occupational group, regardless of strivings to be fair or of attempts to camouflage by polite considerateness. It must be emphasized, however, that competitiveness, and the potential hostility that accompanies it, pervades all human relationships. Competitiveness is one of the predominant factors in social relationships. It pervades the relationships between men and men, between women and women, and whether the point of competition be popularity, competence, attractiveness or any other social value it greatly impairs the possibilities of reliable friendship. It also, as already indicated, disturbs the relations between men and women, not only in the choice of the partner but in the entire struggle with him for superiority. It pervades school life. And perhaps most important of all, it pervades the family situation, so that as a rule the child is inoculated with this germ from the very beginning. The rivalry between father and son, mother and daughter, one child and another, is not a general human phenomenon but is the response to culturally conditioned stimuli. It remains one of Freud's great achievements to have seen the role of rivalry in the family, as expressed in his concept of the Oedipus complex and in other hypotheses. It must be added, however, that this rivalry itself is not biologically conditioned but is a result of given cultural conditions and, furthermore, that the family situation is not the only one to stir up rivalry, but that the competitive stimuli are active from the cradle to the grave.

The potential hostile tension between individuals results in a constant generation of fear—fear of the potential hostility of others, reinforced by a fear of retaliation for hostilities of one's own. Another important source of fear in the normal individual is the prospect of failure. The fear of failure is a realistic one because, in general, the chances of failing are much greater than those of succeeding, and because failures in a competitive society entail a realistic frustration of needs. They mean not only economic insecurity, but also loss of prestige and all kinds of emotional frustrations.

Another reason why success is such a fascinating phantom is its effects on our self-esteem. It is not only by others that we are valued according to the degree of our success; willy-nilly our own self-evaluation follows the same pattern. According to existing ideologies success is due to our own intrinsic merits, or in religious terms, is a visible sign of the grace of God; in reality it is dependent on a number of factors independent of our control—fortuitous circumstances, unscrupulousness, and the like. Nevertheless, under the pressure of the existing ideology, even the most normal person is constrained to feel that he amounts to something when successful, and is worthless if he is defeated. Needless to say, this presents a shaky basis for self-esteem.

All these factors together—competitiveness and its potential hostilities between fellow-beings, fears, diminished self-esteem—result psychologically in the individual feeling that he is isolated. Even when he has many contacts with others, even when he is happily married, he is emotionally isolated. Emotional isolation is hard for anyone to endure; it becomes a calamity, however, if it coincides with apprehensions and uncertainties about one's self.

It is this situation which provokes, in the normal individual of our time, an intensified need for affection as a remedy. Obtaining affection makes him feel less isolated, less threatened by hostility and less uncertain of himself. Because it corresponds to a vital need, love is overvalued in our culture. It becomes a phantom—like success—carrying with it the illusion that it is a solution for all problems. Love itself is not an illusion—although in our culture it is most often a screen for satisfying wishes that have nothing to do with it—but it is made an illusion by our expecting much more of it than it can possibly fulfill. And the ideological emphasis that we place on love serves to cover up the factors which create our exaggerated need for it. Hence the individual—and I still mean the normal individual—is in the dilemma of needing a great deal of affection but finding difficulty in obtaining it.

The situation thus far represents a fertile ground for the development of neuroses. The same cultural factors that affect the normal person—leading him toward a shaky self-esteem, potential hostile tension, apprehensiveness, competitiveness entailing fear and hostility, enhanced need for satisfactory personal relations—affect the neurotic to a higher degree and in him the same results are merely intensified—a crushed self-esteem, destructiveness, anxiety, enhanced competitiveness entailing anxiety and destructive impulses, and excessive need for affection.

When we remember that in every neurosis there are contradictory tendencies which the neurotic is unable to reconcile, the question arises as to whether there are not likewise certain definite contradictions in our culture, which underlie the typical neurotic conflicts. It would be the task of the sociologist to study and describe these cultural contradictions. It must suffice for me to indicate briefly and schematically some of the main contradictory tendencies.

The first contradiction to be mentioned is that between competition and success on the one hand, and brotherly love and humility on the other. On the one hand everything is done to spur us toward success, which means that we must be not only assertive but aggressive, able to push others out of the way. On the other hand we are deeply imbued with Christian ideals which declare that it is selfish to want anything for ourselves, that we should be humble, turn the other cheek, be yielding. For this contradiction there are only two solutions within the normal range: to take one of these strivings seriously and discard the other; or to take both seriously with the result that the individual is seriously inhibited in both directions.

The second contradiction is that between the stimulation of our needs and our factual frustrations in satisfying them. For economic reasons needs are constantly being stimulated in our culture by such means as advertisements, "conspicuous consumption," the ideal of "keeping up with the Joneses." For the great majority, however, the actual fulfillment of these needs is closely restricted. The psychic consequence for the individual is a constant discrepancy between his desires and their fulfillment.

Another contradiction exists between the alleged freedom of the individual and all his factual limitations. The individual is told by society that he is free, independent, can decide his life according to his own free will; "the great game of life" is open to him, and he can get what he wants if he is efficient and energetic. In actual fact, for the majority of people all these possibilities are limited. What has been said facetiously of the impossibility of choosing one's parents can well be extended to life in general—choosing and succeeding in an occupation, choosing ways of recreation, choosing a mate. The result for the individual is a wavering between a feeling of boundless power in determining his own fate and a feeling of entire helplessness.

These contradictions embedded in our culture are precisely the conflicts which the neurotic struggles to reconcile: his tendencies toward aggressiveness and his tendencies toward yielding; his excessive demands and his fear of never getting anything; his striving toward self-aggrandizement and his feeling of personal helplessness. The difference from the normal is merely quantitative. While the normal person is able to cope with the difficulties without damage to his personality, in the neurotic all the conflicts are intensified to a degree that makes any satisfactory solution impossible.

It seems that the person who is likely to become neurotic is one who has experienced the culturally determined difficulties in an accentuated form, mostly through the medium of childhood experiences, and who has consequently been unable to solve them, or has solved them only at great cost to his personality. We might call him a stepchild of our culture.

249